KUWAIT

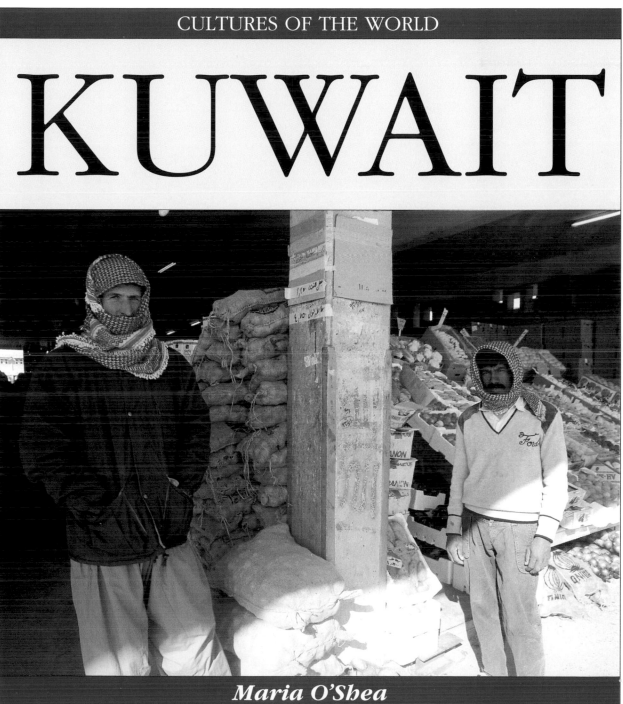

Maria O'Shea

MARSHALL CAVENDISH
New York • London • Sydney

Reference edition published 1999 by
Marshall Cavendish Corporation
99 White Plains Road
Tarrytown
New York 10591

© Times Editions Pte Ltd 1999

Originated and designed by
Times Books International, an imprint of
Times Editions Pte Ltd

Printed in Malaysia

Library of Congress Cataloging-in-Publication Data:

O'Shea, Maria.
    Kuwait / Maria O'Shea.
        p. cm.—(Cultures of the World)
    Includes bibliographical references (p.   ) and index.
    Summary: Describes the geography, history, religious
beliefs, government, and people of Kuwait, a small country on
the Persian Gulf.
    ISBN 0-7614-0871-1 (library binding)
    1. Kuwait—Juvenile literature. [1. Kuwait] I. Title.
II. Series.
DS247.K807   1999
953.67—dc21   98–25833
                    CIP
                    AC

INTRODUCTION

KUWAIT, A TINY STATE in the Arabian Gulf, is surrounded by large and powerful neighbors, Iraq and Saudi Arabia. Despite a small population of about 1.95 million, a large number of them foreigners, the country has managed to forge an identity of its own. Its history is mainly that of the ruling emir's efforts to maintain autonomy, relying largely on alliances and diplomacy. Initially a trading center, the discovery of oil allowed Kuwait to become enormously wealthy. Since gaining independence from Great Britain in 1961, Kuwait has been noted for its farsighted investment of its oil wealth and for its charitable activities in the developing world. Since the 1990 Iraqi invasion, part of this wealth has gone toward rebuilding the country from the ravages of the military occupation. *Cultures of the World—Kuwait* explores the past and present of Kuwait, a small and fascinating country in a volatile region of the world.

CONTENTS

The Fatima Mosque, with its dome, crescent, and minaret, is an excellent example of a traditional mosque.

CONTENTS

A Kuwaiti in white, a cool color for the high desert temperatures.

GEOGRAPHY

KUWAIT LIES AT THE NORTHWEST CORNER of the long, narrow waters of the Persian or Arabian Gulf. To the east the country is bounded by the Gulf, to the north and west by a hostile Iraq, and to the south and southeast by the vast Kingdom of Saudi Arabia. Kuwait has nine islands, of which the two most important, in terms of oil reserves and archeological sites, are Bubiyan and Faylakah. In the south lies the Neutral Zone between Kuwait and Saudi Arabia. This was partitioned, and Kuwait administers the northern zone.

Kuwait is a very small country surrounded by much larger neighbors. From north to south it extends 124 miles (200 km), and from east to west, 105 miles (170 km). It is approximately the size of Hawaii or slightly smaller than Connecticut. Only in the east does Kuwait have no immediate neighbor, although the Persian Gulf is also bounded by other larger states.

The sea that separates Kuwait and the other Arab Gulf states from Iran in the north is most properly known as the Persian Gulf. However, especially since the Iran-Iraq War (1979–90), many Arabs resent this name and prefer to call it the Arabian Gulf. The US State Department calls it the Persian Gulf, but many diplomats feel it is safer to refer to the sea, as well as the region, as "the Gulf."

Opposite: **Sheep enjoying a bit of pasture in the desert. Some land around oases is cultivated.**

Left: **The sea provides drinking water once it is desalinized.**

DESERT AND SEASHORE

Kuwait can be divided into four geographic zones: the desert plateau in the west; a desert plain, covering most of the country; salt marshes and saline depressions that cover most of Kuwait Bay; and an eastern area of coastal dunes. The country consists of gently undulating desert that gradually rises away from the sea to a maximum height of 655 feet (200 m) in the northwest and 985 feet (300 m) in the west.

The terrain varies from firm clay and gravel in the north to loose sandy ground in the south. The plain is an arid steppe desert, and except in the northeast, there are few sand dunes. There are no rivers, lakes, or mountains, but the flatness is relieved by shallow depressions and a few low hills, such as Ahmadi Hill at 450 feet (137 m) in the south and Jal al-Zour ridge at 476 feet (145 m) on the north side of Kuwait Bay. The coastline in the north and around Kuwait Bay consists mainly of mud flats, while there are many fine beaches in the south.

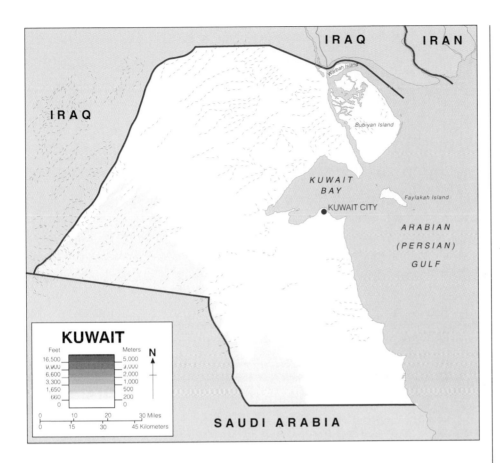

IRAQ

IRAN

IRAQ

Warbah Island

Bubiyan Island

KUWAIT
BAY

Faylakah Island

KUWAIT CITY

ARABIAN
(PERSIAN)
GULF

KUWAIT

Feet		Meters	N
16,500		5,000	
9,900		3,000	
6,600		2,000	
3,300		1,000	
1,650		500	
660		200	
0		0	

| 0 | 10 | 20 | 30 Miles |
| 0 | 15 | 30 | 45 Kilometers |

SAUDI ARABIA

Kuwait Bay is one of only two generously sized natural harbors in the northern half of the Arabian Gulf; the other is in Bahrain. This makes Kuwait ideally positioned to provide access for trade entering and leaving the hinterland of northeast Arabia and Iraq. Before the discovery of oil, Kuwait Bay was the country's most valuable resource. Today, as the location of Kuwait's main commercial port, its economic importance continues.

NOMADS AND BORDERS

As there are no mountains, rivers, or other natural obstacles, Kuwait was for a long time a transit area for nomadic tribes and caravans that moved freely over the desert. This made it difficult to agree on the boundaries separating countries in the area. There was much dispute over this, resulting in boundary problems with Saudi Arabia and Iraq.

In 1922, the British negotiated an agreement on the Kuwaiti-Saudi Arabia border. This led to the creation of a compromise Neutral Zone, which was formally divided between the two countries in 1969. Kuwait's northern frontier with Iraq was agreed upon in 1923 but Iraqi claims on Kuwaiti territory continued: in 1938, the year oil was discovered in Kuwait, and again in 1961 when Britain recognized Kuwait's independence.

Above: **From July to October, Kuwait experiences high humidity and sandstorms. Rainfall rarely exceeds 3.2 inches (8 cm) a year. Even in the winter, the temperature hovers between 45°F (7°C) and 65°F (18°C).**

Right: **In the spring and fall, many birds make Kuwait a stopping point in their seasonal migrations.**

CLIMATE AND WEATHER

The climate of Kuwait is typical of desert regions but is modified by the 180-mile (290 km) long coastline. Kuwait has a harsh desert climate with long, hot summers and temperatures as high as 115°F (46°C) and a daily average temperature of 110°F (43°C). There are four seasons. Summers are long, hot, and dry; winters are short and cool, occasionally cold, with rare sudden showers and storms. Directional winds are seasonal: hot and dry from the north, and warm and humid from the south.

Rainfall is unpredictable, with as little as 0.87 inch (2 cm) in one year to as much as 13.9 inches (35 cm) in another, averaging less than 3.2 inches (8 cm) a year. Dust storms occur throughout the year but are more common in the spring and summer. Humidity is usually low, except in the late summer. Temperatures average 113°F (45°C) in the summer, and 47°F

THE SEASONS IN KUWAIT

Spring

Early spring	Feb 16–April 8	Mild and pleasant, cool at night
Mid-spring	April 9–May 13	Very changeable
Late spring	May 14–May 20	Getting warmer, with hot winds

Summer

Transitional	May 21–Jun 5	Temperatures rising
Dry period	June 6–July 19	Very hot, with scorching winds and sandstorms
Humid period	July 20–Aug 30	Temperatures peak but humidity rises
Transitional	Sep 1–Nov 4	Temperatures dropping but humidity is high
Autumn	Nov 5–Dec 5	Mild and pleasant, sometimes cloudy, cool at night
Winter	Dec 6–Feb 15	Cold, northwesterly winds, cloudy with occasional rain

The nomadic Bedouin ("be-DOO-een") Arabs adjusted their lifestyle over the centuries to cope with the extreme desert climate. This adjustment is reflected in their tents, economic patterns, and clothing. Although most are now settled in houses, it is possible to learn much from them about how to live comfortably in the desert.

(8°C) in the winter. The highest recorded temperature is 125°F (52°C) and the lowest is 42°F (6°C). The daily fluctuation is wide, especially in the desert where the nights can be very cold, even in the summer.

HARDLY A DROP TO DRINK

The lack of fresh drinking water has always been a serious problem in Kuwait. There are few naturally occurring water sources, and the water is mostly brackish and salty. Most of the water can be used for irrigation and cleaning, however. Even before the oil era, Kuwait imported fresh drinking water from Iraq. A good source of drinking water was not discovered until the late 1950s at ar-Rawdatain and Umm al-Aish in the north. This underground reservoir contains possibly 40 billion gallons (182 billion liters) and is the only source of fresh water in the country. The bulk of Kuwait's water comes from the sea and is processed at desalination plants near Mina Abdullah, to make it fit to drink.

Although carried out at great expense, vegetable farming in Wafra helps to reduce the country's dependence on imports of food. Only 1% of the land in Kuwait is cultivated.

WHEN THE DESERT BLOOMS

Although vegetable gardens were once cultivated on parts of the coastal strip, and date palms and fruit trees were once the pride of al-Jahrah, at the western end of Kuwait Bay, farming has always been very marginal to the economy. The immense effort involved in farming in such arid conditions, using limited water supplies, means it is always cheaper to import most food. As the Kuwaiti government is concerned about the country's dependence on the outside world, some areas of the desert have been irrigated, and farming is practiced at great financial cost, notably in Wafra, Sulaibya, and Abdali.

Flora in Kuwait is sparse and there is little regular rain. The soil is mostly sand, and often salty. The desert is scattered with patches of coarse, weedy grass and small, bell-shaped bushes. The country has up to 400 types of vegetation, and a good rainfall in the winter can produce an abundant growth of lush grass and wildflowers; these quickly wither and die.

ANIMAL LIFE

The desert contains many rodents, lizards, and other small animals, but the rabbits, wolves, and gazelles that once roamed the desert have been hunted to near-extinction. There is some pasture for sheep, goats, and camels. These animals may appear to wander wild, but they actually belong to the Bedouin tribes. Although Kuwait has only 20 native species of birds, mostly larks, over 300 types of birds pass through in the spring and fall on their annual migrations, using Kuwait as a stop-off point. At certain times of the year pink flamingos can be seen on the salt flats to the north of Kuwait City.

The waters of the Gulf are very salty and warm, with temperatures ranging from 54–97°F (12–36°C). More than 200 species of fish can be found in the local waters, as well as dolphins, porpoises, whales, and sea-snakes. Many types of shellfish can be found along the shores of Kuwait, as well as in beds deep under the sea.

Less important than they used to be in the past, camels are still very much part of the desert scene.

Kuwait City is a bustling metropolis and the center of government, commerce, and social activities.

KUWAITI CITIES

With its small size and a population of almost two million, Kuwait has a population density of 283 people per square mile (109 per square km), over three times that of the United States. Over 90% of the population of Kuwait live along a coastal belt about 6 miles (10 km) wide, stretching from al-Jahrah at the western edge of Kuwait Bay, to Mina Abdullah in the south. This is known as the Metropolitan Area.

The rest of Kuwait is only very sparsely populated. The Kuwaiti government plans to build new cities in the west, northeast, and south to absorb any population increase and to relieve pressure on the Metropolitan Area. Of Kuwait's nine islands, only Faylakah is inhabited. The 6,000 people who live on the island are supplied with electricity and water by underwater pipes and cables from Kuwait City. Before the Iraqi invasion in 1990, the island was a well-developed tourist resort, accessible by boat from the mainland.

The main cities are Kuwait City, located on the site of the original fort settlement at the southwestern tip of Kuwait Bay; al-Jahrah, an old agricultural town to the west; and al-Salmiya, to the east of the bay. These cities and the southern coastal cities of Mina al-Ahmadi and Mina Abdullah have merged and are linked and encircled by a network of over 2,500 miles (4,023 km) of expressways. Only five other populated areas really exist outside of the Metropolitan Area: the oil towns of al-Abdaliya, as Subayhiyah, and Wafra, and the ports of al-Khiran and Mina Sa'ud, all to the south and west.

The area originally known as Kuwait City, which is the seat of the government and the National Assembly, is a small parcel of land, 2,000 acres (810 hectares), or one-tenth the size of Manhattan Island, New York. The emir's palace and most offices of banks and investment firms are found here. The city and its suburbs have been rebuilt since the 1950s in a series of master plans. The area was zoned into business and residential areas divided by ring roads, which expand outward in concentric circles.

A dilapidated housing complex. Kuwait has distinct residential zones for the different communities.

RESIDENTIAL ZONES

After independence, all citizens were granted free housing. The residential areas of Kuwait City were allocated according to tribal, racial, and religious group. So it is that certain areas are inhabited by Shi'ite Muslims or Bedouins, and others by long-settled, tribal Arabs. The various immigrant communities and expatriates were also allocated housing in distinct districts. All 16 residential zones have their own social amenities, such as shopping malls, mosques, libraries, health centers, banks, restaurants, and cafés. There is not much need for people to move outside their zone, except perhaps to work, and they are often reluctant to do so because of the bad traffic conditions. The urban lifestyle thus reinforces the tribal, class, racial, and religious divisions that exist in Kuwait.

MINA AL-AHMADI, THRIVING IN THE DESERT

Mina al-Ahmadi was Kuwait's first oil town, founded over 40 years ago. Although it now lies in the Metropolitan Area, it is still noted for its greenery, pleasant gardens, and villas on tree-lined avenues. Before Kuwait City's massive expansion and the construction of the expressway, Mina al-Ahmadi was a 45-minute car journey across the desert from the capital. It was a popular place to spend a relaxing day, picnicking in the parks. The town was founded by the Kuwait Oil Company, and the green surroundings were considered to be essential for the morale of employees. A great deal of damage was inflicted on both the town and its complex irrigation system during the Iraqi invasion but Mina al-Ahmadi has been restored, and once again is the garden oasis town of Kuwait.

Mina al-Ahmadi is a coastal town in the south of the country. Built on oil wealth, it is also well-known as a green haven.

HISTORY

KUWAIT IS A VERY NEW COUNTRY, and yet, compared to many of the other Gulf states, Kuwaitis have a long-standing and well-developed sense of unique identity. This is due in part to formal attempts by the government to fashion such an identity and also to the nature of the country's past.

Despite its short history, Kuwait has always been relatively independent and distinct from its neighbors. Its traditional dependence on trade with the rest of the world ensured that Kuwaitis were exposed to many cultures, and this helped foster a distinct identity, as well as enriching Kuwaiti culture.

The trading and seafaring life meant that men could be absent for up to half a year; those left behind became dependent on each other for support. This created a powerful sense of community, which at least partially survived the oil boom.

Kuwaiti history was one of almost uninterrupted economic success until the Iraqi invasion of 1990, from which the country has yet to recover economically, socially, or politically. Also, wartime experiences, both in Kuwait and abroad, led many Kuwaitis to have a new outlook on how Kuwait should be governed.

Wealth generated from trading has given way to wealth from oil and investments, but the same groups of tribes and families have continued to profit. To a large extent, Kuwaiti history is also that of certain families, who founded the country 300 years ago and continue to govern it in the face of increasing challenges and growing Western influence.

Above: **An Iraqi tank is the centerpiece of a war memorial.**

Opposite: **Captured Iraqi tanks stand as a reminder of the invasion of Kuwait in 1990.**

ALEXANDER THE GREAT AND KUWAIT

Alexander the Great conquered most of the Middle East before his early death at the age of 33 in 323 B.C. Greek historians described the many journeys of Alexander the Great and his companions, including the establishment of a garrison on an island in the Persian Gulf named Icarus; this occurred shortly before Alexander's death. From archeological explorations carried out in the 1960s, it has become clear that the Kuwaiti island of Faylakah is the legendary island of Icarus. Although Alexander died three days before his planned conquest of Arabia, Icarus remained an outpost of the Selucid kingdom, which was based in Syria. During this time, it prospered as a trading center until it was overrun by the Parthians, becoming part of Persia but ceasing to have any importance.

Archeologists believe that Faylakah was a holy island, a place of pilgrimage possibly 3,000 years ago for the Sumerians of Mesopotamia, a land that now constitutes the greater part of Iraq. When Faylakah was first discovered by a general of Alexander the Great, its sanctuary and shrines to Artemis, the goddess of hunting, were noted. The island contains Kuwait's richest archeological sites, with Greek temples and fortresses and three Bronze Age settlements.

OLD KUWAIT

Three hundred years ago, the area of Kuwait City was an uninhabited headland jutting into the northwest corner of the Persian Gulf. The town of Kuwait was built in 1716 by members of the Bani Khalid ("bahn-ee KHAHL-eed") tribe, in the early 18th century the dominant tribe of northeastern Arabia. It was called Grane until the mid-19th century. Kuwait is a diminutive of the word *kut* ("kuht"), meaning castle or fort. A scattering of nomadic families lived along the shore with their camels.

The Bani Utub ("bahn-ee U-tob") tribe, a loosely connected group of interrelated families who came to Kuwait from central Arabia, also arrived in the early 18th century. Having been forced into migration by famine in the late 17th century, they traveled via Qatar, establishing a group identity along the way, and in effect establishing a new tribe, the Bani Utub. Once settled in Kuwait, they lived by pearl diving, boat building, and trading.

The settlement became an important port of call for the desert caravans transporting Indian goods from the Persian Gulf to Aleppo in Syria. By the end of the 19th century the town had a population of 10,000 people. A majority of the men were involved in seafaring trades.

Ancient times revisited at Faylakah Island, which has many Bronze Age and Greek archeological sites, ancient sanctuaries, and the remains of pottery and artifacts from up to 4,000 years ago.

THE CARAVAN TRADE

A caravan, with as many as 5,000 camels, could travel from Kuwait to Aleppo in Syria in 70 days. The Sheikh of Kuwait could arrange for these caravans to travel safely, without risk of a raid by Bedouin bandits, in the vicinity of Kuwait and beyond. As well as handling and assisting these traders, the city grew as new trades sprang up to serve the travelers and to meet the needs of the Bedouins who visited the town *souks* ("sooks") or markets, and the townspeople themselves.

Kuwait in the days before the oil boom. Trading and pearl diving were the mainstays of the economy.

KUWAIT DEVELOPS AS A CITY-STATE

By the mid-18th century, the al-Sabahs had become the leading political rulers, a position they still hold. The tribe was responsible for political functions, such as diplomatic and tribal relations and security, while other tribes handled economic and trading matters. Kuwait's small size meant that diplomacy and manipulation of local power balances were necessary to keep a degree of independence from the surrounding powers. Thus the al-Sabahs could establish a strong power base at the expense of the other tribes. Sabah I was recognized as the official ruler in the 1750s.

Until World War I, Kuwait, like the rest of the Arabian peninsula and the Arab world, was part of the Ottoman empire ruled from Istanbul in Turkey. In the late 19th century, the Ottomans added most of the Gulf coastal regions to the province of Basra, including Kuwait in 1871. The al-Sabah family agreed to this, despite having ruled Kuwait for 150 years, as long as the ruler was given the title of governor and the al-Sabahs were allowed to administer the country.

BRITAIN AND KUWAIT

About this time, the British became interested in Iraq and the Gulf, as it was an important staging post on the way to India, an important part of the British empire.

A regular steamship service between Basra and Bombay called at Kuwait, and British Indian postal services were available to traders. British interest in the area provided the Kuwaiti rulers with a way to free themselves of Ottoman control, and in 1899, Sheikh Mubarak signed an agreement with Britain. In return for British protection, Kuwait agreed not to dispose of any part of its territory or enter into any relationship with any power other than Britain. In 1913 borders were defined between Kuwait, the Arabian region known as Nejd, and the province of Basra. Although Kuwait was still part of the Ottoman empire, Britain was in control, and the al-Sabah family had to tread carefully to maintain any independence.

Oil in Kuwait has fueled many social changes. In 1936 there were two primary schools in Kuwait; by 1947 there were 19, and by 1958, 30,000 children attended over 90 schools. In 1961 Kuwait had very few graduates; by 1966, it had its own university.

PEARLS TO OIL

Pearls were the oil of earlier times, providing Kuwait's main source of income. However, in the 1930s, the pearling industry went into a decline caused by two factors. The Japanese developed a method of artificial pearl cultivation, while a worldwide economic depression meant a dramatic fall in the demand for pearls in Europe and the United States. By 1945 only five pearling boats were still working in Kuwait out of the 1,800 active at the turn of the century.

Fortunately, oil came to the rescue. Oil was first struck in 1938 and oil exploitation began in earnest after World War II ended. By 1957 Kuwait was the second largest oil exporter in the world, at that time exceeded only by Venezuela. Kuwait, as one of the world's least populated countries, with a population of less than a quarter of a million, was set to become one of the wealthiest.

The oil boom was overseen by the emir, Sheikh Abdullah al-Salem al-Sabah, who died four years after Kuwait's independence in 1961. He transformed the country into a modern state and dramatically improved social conditions.

Allied troops arrive in Saudi Arabia as the Gulf crisis deepens after the invasion of Kuwait.

WARTIME PROMISES

During World War I, Kuwait supported Britain against Ottoman Turkey, which sided with the Germans. In return, the British promised the Kuwaitis an independent state after the war. At the end of the war and the collapse of the Ottoman empire, the British and French divided up the Middle East, including the state of Kuwait, which was formally under British protection. The British gained the sole right to exploit Kuwait's oil. This annoyed the United States, which then began the search for oil in Saudi Arabia. A special relationship continued between Britain and Kuwait until 1961, when Kuwait became officially independent.

BACKGROUND TO THE IRAQI INVASION

The Iraqi invasion of Kuwait in 1990 came about because of history and money. The personality and style of the government of President Saddam Hussein was also a factor. First, the Iraqis always considered the

international boundaries of the Arab countries to have been imposed by the Europeans who occupied the Middle East after World War I, and to be based on incorrect information about historical patterns of settlement. In particular, Iraqis felt Kuwait should rightly be part of Iraq, not only because of historic trading links, but also because Bedouin tribes had always moved between the two countries before the existence of boundaries.

Second, Iraq needed more money to pay for the damage caused by 10 years of war with Iran. The rights to certain oilfields straddling the Iraq-Kuwait boundary were unresolved, and Iraq needed more oil to sell. The Kuwaitis had also made a lot of oil available on the world market, which had caused the price to drop. Iraq had asked Kuwait to reduce the amount of oil it sold to raise oil prices, but Kuwait refused. The Kuwaitis also wanted Iraq to repay the loan incurred when it was at war with Iran. Throughout the summer of 1990, Kuwait and Iraq argued about oil production and prices, the disputed oil wells, and loan repayments. At the same time, the Iraqis moved troops and weapons to the Kuwaiti border.

Retreating Iraqi forces set fire to two-thirds of the Kuwaiti oil wells, which continued to burn uncontrollably for a long time after the war.

Kuwaitis welcoming the arrival of Allied troops on the liberation of Kuwait. Many Kuwaiti women played an active role in the resistance. They would go out into the streets, carrying food, messages, and weapons to the men in hiding, usually hiding these under their robes.

IRAQ INVADES

In 1979 President Saddam Hussein invaded Iran, officially over a border dispute, and received, if not open support, then no retaliatory action from the United States or the United Nations. This past experience, and a conversation with the US ambassador to Iraq, led him to think that another Iraqi invasion would be the best solution to his problems with Kuwait. Most Iraqis felt Kuwaitis were too wealthy and that they should be forced to share that wealth more.

In the middle of the night, on August 2, 1990, Iraqi soldiers and tanks swept into Kuwait. Kuwait's army totalled only 17,000 soldiers with no experience, while the Iraqi army of one million soldiers had the experience of 10 years of war with Iran.

By morning, Iraqi troops controlled Kuwait City. The emir of Kuwait and his close family escaped to Saudi Arabia. Despite a UN resolution asking Iraq to withdraw, the Iraqis proclaimed a transitional, free government. Within a week, American troops began to arrive in Saudi

Arabia, as it was feared that Iraq would extend its invasion to Saudi Arabia. In response, President Saddam Hussein declared Kuwait the 19th province of Iraq. Several Arab states joined the Allied forces to set up Operation Desert Shield, involving 250,000 soldiers, including 200,000 Americans. The operations were aimed at defending Saudi Arabia and encouraging Iraq to withdraw peacefully from Kuwait.

Inside Kuwait, the civilian population was terrorized, and those who resisted were tortured and executed under a harsh military regime. Economic sanctions against Iraq were not working, and it was feared that Iraq's apparent success in Kuwait would embolden it to attack the traditional Arab enemy, Israel. Allied troop strength in Saudi Arabia was increased to 550,000, including 350,000 Americans, while Iraqi forces in Kuwait rose to 600,000.

By January 1991, a diplomatic solution appeared impossible, so on January 17, the Allied forces began Operation Desert Storm—a devastating air bombing campaign against Iraq and occupied Kuwait. On February 24, the ground assault began, and the Allied forces entered both Kuwait and Iraq. Within two days, the Allied troops had reoccupied Kuwait City, and at 8 a.m. on February 28, after 100 hours of fighting, a ceasefire was called.

HOW THE IRAQI INVASION AFFECTED WOMEN

The Iraqi invasion affected the entire region, especially in challenging traditional views of women's roles in society. Kuwaiti women under the occupation were active in the resistance. Also the American women who served in the US Army were highly conspicuous in this conservative region. The Kuwaiti women in exile in Saudi Arabia were seen by the local women as having more freedom. For example, unlike Saudi women, Kuwaiti women can drive cars and work with men. This led to widespread demonstrations by educated Saudi women for more freedom.

A damaged building in Kuwait, one of the many that were wrecked by the Iraqis.

American troops remain strategically stationed throughout the Gulf, and carry out periodic maneuvers, often in response to suspected Iraqi attempts to intimidate Kuwait.

A NEW KUWAIT?

It was hoped that the end of the war would see many changes in the Arab world and the Gulf states, with a greater degree of democracy. Restoring law and order in Kuwait was difficult, with many Kuwaitis suspicious of each other. Suspected collaborators were sought out and punished. The emir was thus able to defer the reintroduction of a democratic constitution. It took less than a year to extinguish the burning oil wells, but for more than two years, mines and booby traps were still being discovered. Since the war, all Kuwaitis have been concerned with rebuilding the country; the leadership with meeting the changed demands of the population.

THE AFTERMATH OF WAR

Kuwait's infrastructure was badly damaged by the Iraqi occupation and the war. It is estimated that US$30 billion will be needed to repair the damage. Looting, both officially and by individual soldiers, was widespread.

28

Goods such as hospital equipment, cars, computers, and valuables were carted away to Iraq, as were valuable antiquities from the museums. Very few houses escaped the looting, and most public offices and facilities, such as schools and the university, were stripped of their contents and wrecked. Many buildings were badly damaged, and the desalination plants, which provide most of Kuwait's water, needed to be rebuilt, as did the airport and the harbors. There were no buses and the telephone network was destroyed. Equipment returned from Iraq was unusable. Bomb damage to the oil installations caused a huge oil slick that harmed marine life and the fishing industry. The Iraqis set fire to 600 of the 950 oil wells in the country; the smoke polluted the whole Gulf region.

Men looking at a stretch of beach that was heavily mined by Iraqi forces. Many Kuwaiti beaches remain unsafe long after the occupation.

Kuwaitis who stayed behind were mostly those who did not have full citizenship, such as the Palestinians, who were afraid to leave in case they would not be allowed to return. After the occupation, even those who were not collaborators still came under suspicion and were expelled or deprived of their residency rights. The Palestinians were singled out for harsh treatment because the Palestinian political leadership had supported the Iraqi government. Without the Palestinians, Kuwait was deprived of a highly skilled and educated workforce.

After liberation, Kuwaitis worked together to restore the country to some degree of normality. The expatriates who were thought to have collaborated with the Iraqis were summarily expelled or refused reentry. The elections in 1992 were a disappointment to many: voting rights were limited, with women still not allowed to vote. The results were widely interpreted as a success for the supporters of increased Islamic law.

GOVERNMENT

THE STATE OF KUWAIT is a constitutional monarchy, ruled by the emir of Kuwait, who must be from the al-Sabah family, descended from the late Mubarak al-Sabah. The emir rules with the help of the consultative institution of the National Assembly, and the bureaucracy. To a large extent, these institutions have been successful in creating a national identity that includes loyalty to the country's leaders. The government has generally encouraged the people of Kuwait to support the "national interest," rather than use force. But the opposition of the 1980s, including Islamicists (people who believe that Islam can provide the best system of government, and that Islamic law should be in place) and the pro-democracy movement, has left the government unsure about its style of ruling. Although the Iraqi invasion helped reinforce a Kuwaiti identity, it also raised many questions about the type of government a liberated Kuwait should have.

Opposite: **The country's flag flies high at Kuwaiti Towers, a landmark that dominates the skyline.**

Left: **The Kuwaiti Parliament Building. Although the country is ruled by the al-Sabah family, there is an elected National Assembly.**

Kuwaitis shopping at a night market. In terms of representation, not many of the people in Kuwait have the right to vote.

THE NATIONAL ASSEMBLY

From its establishment after independence, the 50 elected members of the National Assembly carried on a lively political debate with the government until it was closed between 1976 and 1981 and then dissolved in 1986. Political parties have not been legalized in Kuwait, although National Assembly members have formed opposing groups with certain interests.

The right to vote was originally restricted to a small percentage of the Kuwaiti population. This is still true today, after the reestablishment of the National Assembly. Only male "first class" Kuwaiti citizens over 21 years of age can vote. Active members of the armed forces and the al-Sabah family are barred from voting or serving in the National Assembly. In 1985 only 57,000 Kuwaitis, less than 5% of the total residential population of 1.5 million, could vote.

The first National Assembly tended to criticize the ruling cabinet's ministers and policies. Then it was claimed that the government interfered with the elections in order to ensure that more cooperative assemblies

KEEPING IT IN THE FAMILY

Although the al-Sabah family has ruled Kuwait since the 18th century, the family has ruled as a formal institution only since the mid-20th century. Since independence, the ruling family has always held at least one quarter of all cabinet posts and the most important ministerial posts such as foreign affairs, defense, information, and the interior. There are over 1,200 members of the al-Sabah family, who are themselves divided into various groups depending on their closeness to the ruling line, that is, descendants of the first emir's sons, Jabar and Salem.

Kuwait is a fully independent Arab state with a democratic style of government where sovereignty rests with the nation in the form of the constitution.

were elected, but the members still tended to be critical of the cabinet and oppose certain policies. As the number of disagreements grew, the emir dissolved the assembly in 1976. The government was particularly concerned with the ties that seemed to be developing between the Kuwaiti opposition and groups in the wider Arab world, especially considering the large number of politically active, highly educated Palestinians that were living in Kuwait. Kuwait's neighbor, Saudi Arabia, had never approved of the democratic experiment in Kuwait and encouraged the emir to be wary of such possible challenges to his rule.

The emir claimed that the members of the National Assembly had spent so much time arguing over issues that budgets and new laws were delayed. Certainly the members had made many enemies from their campaigns against corruption and price controls; campaigns that were popular with the people. When the assembly was dissolved, press controls were also introduced, so it is hard to know how unpopular the suspension of the assembly was. It appeared to have been accepted without much complaint.

To everyone's surprise, the emir kept his promise to restore the National Assembly at a time that he judged right, and this was in 1981. The 1979 Iranian revolution concerned the emir, as it demonstrated the dangers of too little democracy and the inability of a strong government to control a dissatisfied population. By encouraging Islamicist candidates to stand for the National Assembly, the emir hoped to include the religious opposition in the government. Excluding them, as Iran had done, could lead to a revolutionary opposition.

THE ISLAMICISTS AND THE EMIR

Islamicists are those who believe that the country should be run as an Islamic state, according to the guidance of the Koran and Islamic law.

Reflecting trends throughout the Middle East, the Islamicist assembly members pressed for the introduction of more Islamic law, less reliance on Western values, and a reappraisal of its support for Iraq in the Iran-Iraq War. Some of these ideas were very popular with the Kuwaiti people, especially with the Shi'ites and many non-Kuwaiti residents, precisely the groups that the government feared most. In the 1985 election, the government encouraged more Bedouin candidates and Kuwaiti nationalists. Despite such efforts, a core of Islamicists still remained and they cooperated with the nationalists to block some government legislation. They also probed into corruption in the cabinet and called for the resignation of two ministers, both prominent al-Sabahs.

At this time, low international oil prices were causing anxiety over Kuwait's economy. The Iran-Iraq War was a source of security concerns, and the Kuwaiti government drew close to its neighbor Saudi Arabia, which disapproved of parliaments and assemblies. The emir feared that the political debates originating in the National Assembly would increase divisions in society, especially between Sunni and Shi'ite Muslims. The Shi'ites were considered to be possible agents of Iranian revolutionary ideas. In 1985 Kuwait experienced a wave of political violence, including, for the first time, an attack on the emir. The emir decided that enough was enough, and the assembly was suspended for the second time.

Although the National Assembly had very limited powers, and it could not select the emir or the cabinet, it was a forum for debate on issues such as oil policy, women's rights, and religion in politics. Its absence meant that there was no real way to force the emir to address certain issues other than through political agitation and opposition activities. Only those who could personally address the emir could raise issues with him.

PROFILES

The present emir is His Highness, Sheikh Jabar al-Ahmad al-Jabar al-Sabah (left), born in 1928 and appointed emir in 1978. Before his appointment, Sheikh Jabar had long served in the government. He was head of security and liaison with the Kuwait Oil Company in the 1950s, head of the Finance Department, and founding director of the Kuwait Fund for Arab Economic Development. After independence he was finance minister, then deputy prime minister and finance minister at the same time. He was prime minister from 1965 until the death of the previous emir in 1977.

The present crown prince (right), and thus future emir, is His Highness Sheikh Saad al-Abdullah al-Salem al-Sabah. Only two years younger than the emir, he was appointed crown prince in 1978, and within a month, prime minister. He is also president of the Supreme Defense Council, the Supreme Petroleum Council, the Civil Service Commission, and the Higher Housing Council. He is the eldest son of the late emir of Kuwait, Sheikh Abdullah al-Salem al-Sabah.

During the Iraqi occupation of Kuwait, the emir promised the Kuwaiti people that they would have the right to hold free elections for the National Assembly. The Kuwaiti definition and practice of democracy is something that has increasingly been challenged by Kuwaitis, especially since the Gulf War, and many Kuwaitis would like to see more democracy introduced at a faster pace.

Kuwait's heavy reliance on foreign workers is a source of great concern to the government. Efforts are being made to train Kuwaitis to take over some of the jobs now being done by foreigners.

THE BUREAUCRACY

The Kuwaiti bureaucracy is one of the largest per capita in the world, all created after the discovery of oil. Kuwait did not have an extensive administration under the British, and oil exploitation makes few bureaucratic demands. The need to spend the oil revenues was the real impetus to expanding this bureaucracy. The system provided pleasant employment for Kuwaitis, who were no longer required in the traditional industries that were displaced by oil wealth.

As there have never been enough educated Kuwaitis to run this giant organization, many Arabs from other countries, in particular the Palestinians, were employed in managerial positions, overseen by Kuwaiti managers or ministers. By 1989 only 44% of civil servants were Kuwaiti. At the senior staff level, the percentage of Kuwaitis was higher, at 66%, after efforts were made to increase the proportion. As only 28% of the population were Kuwaiti citizens at that time, this was an over-representation of Kuwaitis in the civil service.

Kuwait is divided into 25 electoral regions, each of which elects two members to the National Assembly. In October 1992 elections were held for a new assembly. Voting was limited to men over 21 who held first-class Kuwaiti passports. Political parties remained banned, as were public meetings on politics. The public voted for many Islamicist candidates, and 31 of the 50 seats were won by candidates who opposed the government. The cabinet remained the appointees of the emir, and were automatically members of the assembly.

THE MILITARY

Kuwait has always depended on diplomacy to solve problems with its neighbors. The army was always intended to delay an aggressor, while the government rallied diplomatic support. In 1978 Kuwait was the first Gulf state to introduce national conscription and compulsory high school military training. All Kuwaiti men, including the al-Sabahs, between the ages of 18 and 30 had to serve in the army. Previously, the army had relied on Bedouin professionals, commanded by expatriate advisors. In 1980 the Iran-Iraq War led to a call-up of Kuwaiti men up to the age of 50. Despite attempts to make army life more attractive, Kuwaitis were reluctant to serve. On the eve of the Iraqi invasion, the army was only 20,000 strong, mostly non-Kuwaitis, and up to 60% of them were on summer leave.

Kuwaitis are still not attracted to a military career, and the army is only 16,000 strong. Over 13% of the GDP is spent on defense, with the Kuwaitis appearing to rely on technological weaponry and intervention from the United States and other forces in future time of need.

The army is well-funded but lacks strength in numbers. Despite national conscription, Kuwaitis are generally reluctant to be in the military.

A gathering of men often serves more than just a social purpose, as weightier issues of politics or business are discussed.

DIWANIYAH: A FORM OF DEMOCRACY?

It may appear that Kuwait lacks the democratic institutions that are necessary for the emir to make decisions reflecting public opinion. This is true in that women are officially unrepresented, as are expatriates and those who are denied full citizenship. However, Kuwait has a traditional institution—the *diwaniyah* ("dee-WAHN-ee-yah")—that allows Kuwaiti men, and some women, to debate and discuss their opinions and to channel these views to their rulers. When Kuwait was a small city-state, this system ensured that most Kuwaitis could express their views. The diwaniyah system ensured that Kuwait was a fairly democratic society where all opinions were valued.

The diwaniyah is a social gathering for men, traditionally held in a special reception room, also called a diwaniyah. These meetings are usually held weekly and are attended, by invitation, by groups of male friends and relatives who discuss business and politics over coffee, or maybe a meal. They are an occasion for many social and business activities

Diwaniyah: A Form of Democracy?

and also a way of establishing contact with people who can carry their concerns and opinions to the ears of the cabinet members, or even to the emir himself.

Most people attend several diwaniyahs, meeting different groups of people. In this way, common concerns will be discussed and conveyed to the highest diwaniyahs. When the National Assembly was closed, the emir encouraged the diwaniyah network as an alternative to elected assemblies. The network fueled the pro-democracy movement in Kuwait and was instrumental in the resistance to the Iraqi occupation.

The diwaniyah system works well for male Kuwaiti citizens who are admitted to this network. Women have attempted to create their own networks, but they are, except at the highest social level, excluded from political decision-making. The diwaniyahs allow them some influence over certain areas, such as education, where many women have senior positions. They may also express some opinions through their male relatives, who might raise their concerns. Non-Kuwaitis may have their own networks, but these are unlikely to overlap with those of Kuwaitis.

From the word, diwan ("dee-WAHN"), Arabic for a reception room, we get the word divan, a low bed or couch. This is because these rooms were traditionally furnished with mattresses and cushions, so that many people could sit or lounge on the floor comfortably.

AN INDIRECT BUT EFFICIENT ROUTE

An example of the efficient but complex working of the diwaniyah network might be that of Abdullah, who finds that his construction business is badly affected by a shortage of Filipino workers because of government restrictions on the numbers admitted into Kuwait. He expresses his problems at a family diwaniyah. His cousin, who works in the Ministry of Defense, agrees with him. At a diwaniyah of army officers and their friends, which he regularly attends, he raises this concern. A fellow guest, who is the husband of the sister of a cabinet minister, then agrees to raise the matter at his family diwaniyah. Thus the matter is brought to the attention of a cabinet minister, who might then discuss it with his colleagues. If several of them have also heard of this problem, they will formulate a policy to deal with it.

ECONOMY

THE ECONOMY OF KUWAIT shares a great similarity with that of its neighbors. The economies of the Gulf region are distinct from those of third world countries and from those of advanced countries, with which they appear to share a similar or higher standard of living. A per capita income of US$16,900 (US per capita income is US$22,000) conceals both serious income inequalities between Kuwaitis and expatriates, as well as the hidden income in the form of welfare benefits given to all Kuwaitis.

The first and most obvious distinction is the economy's dependence on a single product, petroleum. A second distinctive feature of economies like that of Kuwait's is that income from the export of oil is paid directly to the government. The Kuwaiti government, therefore, has to manage this income within the domestic economy. A third way in which oil-exporting countries like Kuwait are unique is that most state income is earned in foreign exchange, which can only be put to certain uses.

Kuwait has few natural resources other than oil. The Arabian-Iranian basin, which stretches down through the Gulf, contains 65% of the world's oil reserves. Kuwait lies entirely within this basin, so in effect, Kuwait is floating on a sea of oil. As the oil lies close to the surface, extraction costs are among the lowest in the world. Kuwait has around 1% of the world's natural gas reserves.

Left: A shopkeeper stands before his wares in a market.

Opposite: **Although less important than it used to be, fishing, especially for prawns and shrimp, is still widely practiced.**

41

At the end of 1995, the nationalities of the labor force were as follows: Kuwaitis, 16.6% Bedoons, 1.7% Arab expatriates, 27.9% Non-Arab expatriates, 53.8%

TOO RICH TOO FAST?

Like its neighbors, Kuwait has been unable to solve the question of how to spend its oil income in ways to develop the country. Imported goods and services require a skilled, local labor force, able management, and a strong commercial structure if they are to be used effectively. Kuwait's excess of foreign exchange has resulted in the development of a slave economy, in which goods and services, together with the labor to run them, are imported. Meanwhile Kuwaitis live like masters without serious productive employment. Before 1990 more than 75% of the Kuwaiti labor force were foreign nationals.

Per capita income represented by the value of oil exports divided by the number of citizens is extremely high. Generally, a low-quality labor force that demands high incomes is a poor basis for establishing competitive agriculture or industry. In short, Kuwaitis will not work for less money than they can receive from the government simply by being Kuwaiti citizens. To produce things in Kuwait would be expensive, as the wages for Kuwaitis would be too high. Apart from very expensive items such as jewelry, or bulky items such as furniture, it is cheaper to import most goods from countries where wages are lower.

DUTCH DISEASE

Most oil economies in the Gulf tend to suffer from a condition called Dutch Disease. This occurs when the economy outside the oil sector is undermined by the easy living gained from oil exports. The term stems from the problems faced by the Dutch economy when natural gas was discovered and exploited for the first time. Welfare provision grew, and government employment expanded unnecessarily as the state controlled the oil income. Establishing alternative ways of earning money was neglected.

BLACK GOLD

Oil was first discovered in 1938, but the first exports were not made until 1946. Kuwait benefited from the closure of the Iranian oilfields in 1951 during a period of political unrest, as well as from the discovery of new oilfields at Mina al-Ahmadi. By 1953 Kuwait had the largest output of all the countries in the Gulf area. Its production was not overtaken by any of its neighbors until 1965.

Kuwait has followed a policy of extracting, refining, and retailing oil. This means that it is able to sell higher priced products rather than lower priced crude oil. By the mid-1980s, 80% of Kuwait's crude oil was refined locally, and 250,000 barrels per day of refined oil were sold as gasoline from 4,400 Kuwaiti-owned gas stations in Europe, under the Q8 logo.

Kuwait has its own tanker fleet to export the oil. It is also involved in the extraction and refining of oil in other countries and has a well-developed petrochemical industry that uses oil by-products.

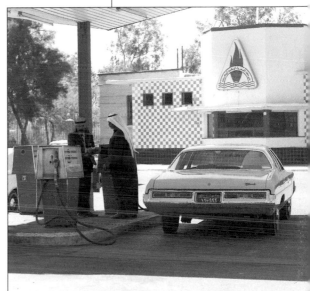

The price of oil is lower in real terms now than in 1970, and oil is being consumed three times faster than new discoveries are made.

THE HIGH COST OF WAR

The cost of repairing damage to the oil industry sustained during the Iraqi invasion and occupation has been estimated at approximately US$1 billion. When the Iraqis left, 600 of Kuwait's 950 oil wells were ablaze, and another 80 were flowing uncontrollably, causing a loss of four to six million barrels of oil a day. Massive damage had also been inflicted on tanks, pipelines, terminals, pumping stations, and the three refineries. Post-liberation production has been built up to and maintained at around 1.5 million barrels a day, higher than before the invasion, to recoup Kuwait's immense losses, and to rebuild the country.

The Kuwaiti stock exchange, which suffered a bad crash in 1982.

WHAT IF THE OIL RUNS OUT?

Oil is a limited product, as is the gas that accompanies it. Kuwait has an estimated 96 billion barrels of oil left, which at the current rates of extraction will last for more than 100 years. Only Iraq and Saudi Arabia have greater reserves. Nevertheless, the Kuwaiti government has long been aware that future generations of Kuwaitis will not be able to rely on a massive oil income. With this in mind, the government embarked on an ambitious policy to protect Kuwait's future.

Kuwait decided in the mid-1970s not to attempt to diversify its economy but to concentrate instead on refining and exploration techniques. Oil production was kept low to maintain output, and financial resources were invested abroad for future generations. Only 10% of Kuwaiti oil is used within the country, as it is considered too valuable to burn. The laws to protect Kuwait's future generations oblige the government to invest 10% of oil revenues in long-term investments, mostly abroad. These investments account for half the total revenue generated in Kuwait. Nearly 70% of this income is not spent, but reinvested. Daily income from these investments is currently about US$20 million. The government owns many commercial ventures around the world, including leisure facilities in the United States such as the Phoenician Resort Hotel in Scotsdale, Arizona. Kuwait has substantial holdings in most of the New York Stock Exchange's leading 100 corporations, as well as in most European countries.

Thanks to these extensive investments outside the Middle East, the Kuwaiti government was able to function, without resorting to borrowing, during the Iraqi invasion and the time that it took to restart oil production.

OPEC

The Organization of Petroleum Exporting Countries was established in 1960 by five oil-producing countries as a reaction to the policies of the large international oil companies. The five—Iraq, Iran, Venezuela, Saudi Arabia, and Kuwait—were producing 85% of the world's oil. OPEC aimed to raise international oil prices and increase the share of profits that the producing states received. OPEC's membership grew to 13 countries, which included most of the Arab Gulf states. Kuwait later joined the Organization of Arab Petroleum Exporting Countries (OAPEC), which had a more political agenda. In the 1970s OAPEC boycotted Israel and its supporting countries and raised oil prices by 70%, causing a world oil crisis. OPEC and OAPEC have allowed countries like Kuwait to bargain for favorable oil prices and to agree on production levels to maintain those prices. The Iraqi invasion of Kuwait illustrated that not all of the members agree on production levels and prices.

Kuwait's oil production in 1972 reached 3.3 million barrels of oil a day, which was gradually reduced to around one million barrels a day before the 1990 Iraqi invasion. This was a result of both lower world demand due to energy conservation and Kuwait's desire to conserve its supplies. This meant a decrease of 66% in oil revenues over 18 years, which was offset by Kuwait's overseas investments.

The financial district of Kuwait City. Overseas investment is the most important non-petroleum sector.

A RENTIER ECONOMY

Economists and political scientists call oil economies like that of Kuwait's rentier economies. In a rentier economy, the source of income, or rent, is externally generated, involves little contact with the local economy, goes directly to the state, and is very large.

In Kuwait, revenues have historically come from foreign oil companies. The oil industry creates few related industries, generates money rather than jobs, and is capital-intensive, that is, uses money rather than people.

Revenues from oil go to the state, unlike in most countries where income from foreign trade goes to companies that make and export goods. Before oil was discovered, the sheikhs collected taxes on pearling and trading boats.

Now, Kuwaitis do not pay taxes, except some customs duties. The state owns the land where oil is found, or the rights to exploit it, so it also owns the income from oil. Kuwait's oil revenues are around 90% of the country's total revenues.

THE EFFECTS OF OIL DEPENDENCY

Kuwait's rentier economy has affected the nature of the Kuwaiti state in certain ways. A rentier state has a different function from that of other states. In most countries the government collects taxes for redistribution. In Kuwait there are no taxes, and the government simply distributes oil revenues through direct transfers, social services, and state jobs. The country has no Internal Revenue Service, but it does have ministries for health, social affairs, and education. It also has a large ministry for oil. The Kuwaiti government can distribute revenue, but it cannot redistribute wealth—that is, it can give to the poor, but it cannot take from the rich. This means that the state has limited economic policy tools, and little flexibility.

Like all rentier economies, oil weakened certain old classes in Kuwait, such as the merchants, because the state no longer needed their taxes and Kuwaitis no longer depended on them for employment. If oil wealth destroyed certain social groups, it also created a new one: a huge class of civil servants and bureaucrats that depends on the state for its existence.

Thus, this type of economy contributes in the long term to a politically unstable state. In Kuwait, the state was initially stable as it created a new social structure. But with no taxation, the government does not need to consider the wishes of the people, because their money is not being spent. Being wealthy also means the government is able to buy the support of some people. (The Kuwaitis have shown, however, that they are no longer content in being simply wealthy but want more say in shaping the country.)

Finally, a rentier economy is dependent on the outside world. Kuwait shows a distinct lack of economic independence. It must rely on foreign markets and the price they are prepared to pay for oil, on foreign labor, and imported goods.

Oil pipelines snaking through the desert. The Kuwaiti government must find a way to spread the benefits of oil to the population at large.

AN OUTWARD FACING ECONOMY

With agriculture never a successful pursuit because of the harsh climate, Kuwaitis have traditionally looked elsewhere—to the desert and the sea for food and even water. In the past, water was imported from Iraq. Long-distance trade and pearling were, until the 1930s, the heart of the economy.

Before oil, Kuwait's economy depended on the movements of the Bedouins and caravans from Baghdad and Aleppo, on the vagaries of Indian and African markets, and on the pearl-purchasing patterns of wealthy Europeans. With oil, this pattern of dependency has deepened. It is cheaper now to import most goods, and as Kuwait is only really accessible by air or sea, this means that supplies are at the mercy of external events. During the Iran-Iraq War, supplies coming in by ship became unreliable, and this affected the availability and prices of consumer goods.

A dhow or Kuwaiti boat laden with cargo. Boat-building, which was once a significant sector of the economy, has declined.

A NAUTICAL TRADITION

The sea was the most important resource in pre-oil Kuwait. It was the main source of food, and many fishing boats operated from Kuwaiti shores. In addition to the pearl-diving crews, 30–40 large Kuwaiti vessels or *dhows* ("dowz") regularly sailed to Africa and India in the early 20th century. Kuwait formed part of an Indian Ocean trade triangle, which linked the Gulf, the western shores of India, and the east coast of Africa. Trade accounts were paid in Indian currency until independence in 1961.

PEARLING

A pearl is a translucent ball formed inside a shellfish. When a piece of grit or sand enters the shell, the shellfish coats it with the glossy mother-of-pearl (calcium carbonate) with which they line their shells, forming a pearl. These natural pearls are usually cream-colored but can be of many shades, including black, green, and blue. They vary in shape and size and at times have been more valuable on the world market than diamonds. This is partly because of the difficulties involved in collecting the pearls. The mother-of-pearl inside the shell can be used to make buttons and other decorative items.

Pearl divers would stuff beeswax into their ears, close their nostrils with a horn pincer, and protect their fingers with leather covers. They would then leap from their boats, a rock tied to their ankle to pull them to the seabed, and gather as many oysters into a basket as they could before they had to come up again for air. About 20 oysters could be collected in the 40-75 seconds that they stayed under. A good diver could dive up to 50 times a day, although it could take many dives to find even one pearl. There was no way to predict the presence of a pearl in a shellfish, so the divers had to depend on their luck in getting the ones with the precious finds. This variety of oyster is not edible, so those without pearls are useless. The divers were not paid a salary but took a share of the profits from the summer pearling voyages, which might travel as far as southern India, where there are large pearl banks.

The work was dangerous—a diver would start at a very young age, when he was very fit, then retire early due to breathing problems, unless he had already been injured or killed by sharks. As the diver had to borrow money in advance from the ship's captain to support his family during the journey, he was already in debt and under pressure to dive many times. The daily routine was long, and the food frugal, consisting mostly of coffee and dates, with some fish. In 1914 Kuwait had 500 pearl-diving crews, providing a living for over 9,000 men.

Cultured pearls are produced by introducing small beads into the shells of oysters living in specially created tanks. Such pearls were known in China for centuries. In the early 20th century, world prices of pearls fell because of an increasing Japanese production of cultured pearls. Although they are less valuable, cultured pearls are extremely easy, cheap, and safe to produce.

A gold craftsman making a piece of jewelry. Many workers in the private sector are non-Kuwaitis.

THE WORLD OF WORK

Employment in Kuwait generally falls into three categories: the government sector (ministries, other public authorities, and the state-owned oil companies), the private sector, and the domestic service. More than 90% of the Kuwaitis in the workforce are employed in the government sector, as every Kuwaiti citizen is guaranteed a job for life. Salaries are high, and Kuwaitis do not like to work for private companies, unless they are owned by their families.

Of the non-Kuwaitis, only 11% work for the government, the majority (69%) work in the private or business sector, and nearly 19% are domestic servants. It is estimated that there is one foreign servant for every four Kuwaitis. Following government plans to reduce the number of foreigners working for the government, less than 40% of government employees are now expatriates (in 1989, the figure was 51%).

Office hours are quite short in the government sector, and this allows many Kuwaitis to have an additional private business in the afternoon. In the private sector there is a long afternoon break; this, together with an early start, is because of the hot weather. Gradually, with air-conditioning, this is being phased out for a regular working day.

During the fasting month of Ramadan, hours are shorter or altered. Generally, ministries and oil companies work from 7 a.m. to 2 p.m., while many companies open from 8 a.m. to 1 p.m., and then again from 4:30 p.m. to 7 p.m. Banks are open from 7:30 a.m. to 2:30 p.m.

TRADING TRADITIONS

The majority of Kuwaitis appear to be involved to some extent in international trade, an activity that has always been their lifeblood. Although oil makes up 90% of exports, which are all in government hands, over US$6 billion worth of imports arrive in Kuwait every year. Many of these are arranged by Kuwaiti or expatriate traders. Other than oil, very little is produced in Kuwait, but Kuwaitis are demanding and discerning consumers. As there are no sales taxes and few import duties, goods can be sold in large volume at reasonable prices. The main sources of imports are the United States (35%), Japan (12%), Italy, Britain, Canada, and France. Imports consist of food, automobiles, building materials, machinery, and textiles. Kuwaitis are keen on the latest technology and most Kuwaitis, even teenagers, have mobile telephones and the latest television sets, video and audio equipment, and computers.

Kuwaitis checking out the latest models in a car showroom. Automobiles are one of the main imports of the oil-rich state.

TRANSPORTATION

Kuwait has no railway, and internal air travel is not really necessary, although helicopters are used by companies and some individuals. Public transportation is limited to taxis and some buses. A railway is planned along the coastal corridor. Also in the works are a coach service to link the new towns and passenger ferries for the islands.

There are over 530,000 motor vehicles, more than one for every four people, and 144,000 commercial vehicles. During the invasion, the Iraqis took away many vehicles and ferries. There is a huge demand for cars now to replace the ones stolen.

KUWAITIS

KUWAIT IS A GULF ARAB SOCIETY. Kuwaitis identify themselves as Arabs from Kuwait and they feel part of the wider Arab world. Kuwait has a common identity with other Gulf Arabs and shares cultural traits with Bahrain, Oman, Qatar, the United Arab Emirates, Saudi Arabia, and Iraq. Gulf Arab culture is a mixture of Islamic and Arab culture, with African, Indian, and Persian influences. Kuwait itself has a distinct identity, forged by the experience of migration and of building the Kuwaiti settlement. More recently the Iraqi invasion also helped shaped this distinctness.

Kuwaiti society, like many societies, is divided by class, wealth, tribal affiliations, religion, and aspirations. Although the majority are descendants of the Bani Utub families who founded Kuwait, some are of other tribal origins, or from other Gulf states or Iran. The reliance on expatriates, or people from another country, has led to Kuwaiti citizens becoming a minority, and this has created serious social problems.

Left: **Kuwaitis possess a distinct identity, shaped by the experiences of early and recent history.**

Opposite: **A shopkeeper sits before his abundant stock of goods.**

A Bedouin camp. Many of its inhabitants are not considered legal residents of Kuwait.

There are around 300,000 Bedoons, one-third of the native population. About half live illegally in Kuwait, while the rest are in exile. Most were born in Kuwait. About 30,000 are married to Kuwaiti women or are children of such a marriage.

KUWAITIS IN THE MINORITY

Most of the people who live in Kuwait are not Kuwaitis but foreign workers, mostly from Asia and the Arab world. In 1957, non-Kuwaitis already made up 45% of the population. Before the Iraqi invasion, they formed up to 75% of the population and over 80% of the workforce. Slightly more than half of these were Asian, the rest mostly Arabs, especially Palestinians, Jordanians, and Egyptians. Palestinians were particularly evident in managerial jobs.

The presence of so many foreigners in the country has been a source of anxiety for Kuwaitis who fear that their culture will be overwhelmed. More than 120 nationalities live in Kuwait, and adherents of almost all religions can be found.

After the Gulf War, attempts were made to reduce the number of foreigners, often by deporting them. Many workers who tried to return from their home countries were denied entry. Now about 60% of the population is non-Kuwaiti.

CITIZENS WITHOUT CITIZENSHIP?

Foreigners who live in Kuwait will never receive the equivalent of a Green Card or Kuwaiti citizenship, but this also applies to many people who would appear to be Kuwaitis. On independence, citizenship was (and still is) dependent on proven Kuwaiti ancestry, with family residence from at least 1920. This was difficult to prove, especially for nomadic tribes, many of whom did not see the importance of citizenship when they had no need of the state. First-class citizenship was given to a third of the native population, another third were given partial or second-class citizenship, and the remaining third were considered potential citizens, *bedoon jinsiyyah* or *bedoons* ("be-DOONS"). Citizens and other inhabitants were clearly separated in all respects, legally and socially. Government payments were restricted to citizens only, but in many other respects, the Bedoons were treated as citizens and always hoped to be recognized as such one day.

Historically, many Bedouin tribes lived on the outskirts of Kuwait City and in the desert beyond. Often, they served as armed retainers to the ruling al-Sabah family. After independence, some Bedouins were offered citizenship in return for military service and support in the assembly. Some collected passports from more than one Gulf state, but others became stateless or Bedoons. Bedoons include Bedouins who lived in the desert in or near Kuwait but had no documentary proof of their residence. Among them were those entitled to citizenship but who were not registered by their parents or grandparents.

Foreigners make up the majority of the population of Kuwait.

SOCIAL DIVISIONS

In Kuwait divisions exist between the very rich and the less rich, and there are very few poor Kuwaiti citizens. There is a social division between the Bani Utub, or merchant families who are descendants of the original founders of Kuwait, like the ruling family, and the rest of the citizenry. Of the latter, one of the biggest distinct social groups is the Bedouins, many of whom are stateless Bedoons.

The ruling al-Sabah family became economically superior after the oil boom; as political rulers, they controlled the revenue. All al-Sabahs receive a monthly check from the civil list. They marry within the family and hold key positions in the government, as well as in most business, educational, and other ventures. In many respects, they are above the law, as any complaints against them are not dealt with by ordinary courts, but by family councils.

A cloth merchant. The merchant class has survived many economic and social changes brought about by oil wealth.

The oil boom changed the class structure dramatically. Kuwait's rentier economy makes access to the state, rather than access to private property, the prime determinant of wealth. Classes such as artisans and those who worked for traders opted for jobs with the state, taking on new identities as bureaucrats and technocrats.

Nevertheless, the merchant class did not disappear. This was because the merchants had established their own culture and interests, with social institutions such as diwaniyahs (social and political gatherings) and marriages between the families. The government found it cheaper and easier to buy their support than to remove them, so the merchant class remained intact as a group.

THE IRAQI INVASION AND NEW DIVISIONS

Within three months of the 1990 Iraqi invasion, 400,000–600,000 of Kuwait's less than 700,000 citizens were abroad, mainly in Saudi Arabia.

After the war, the Kuwaiti government tried to encourage people to return, but many feared the effects of the air pollution from blazing oil wells and were disheartened by the general destruction. Although the invasion had initially unified the Kuwaitis, now a new division emerged between those who had stayed and those who had left during the occupation. The fact that the rulers had been comfortably exiled in Saudi Arabia or in the West, led people to accuse them of being detached from the suffering. It was expected that those who stayed behind, whose views had been changed by their experiences, would form a new political and social alliance to challenge the government. Ultimately, however, the ties of common experience that bound those people were not as powerful as the old loyalties, and the social structure remained barely changed, except for the expatriates and Bedoons who were expelled.

The rulers who had been in Saudi Arabia were affected by the culture and ideals of that country, and returned with more conservative ideas about politics and society, rather than being sympathetic to, for example, women's demands that they be given more equality.

RELIGIOUS DIVISIONS

The constitution of Kuwait recognizes religious freedom, although it forbids attempts to convert Muslims to other religions. The small, mostly expatriate, Christian (8.4%) and Hindu (2%) communities can practice their faiths freely and have their own places of worship. There is also a small Jewish community of merchant families.

The majority of Kuwaitis are Sunni Muslims, but between 10% and 25% are Shi'ite Muslims. The Shi'ite community is diverse and consists of Gulf Arabs who emigrated from Bahrain and Saudi Arabia with short stays in Iran, and Persian Shi'ites who speak Persian and maintain ties to Iran. As they often marry within their community, they have a distinct identity, although they also have a strong Kuwaiti identity.

The Iranian revolution encouraged some Shi'ites to complain of unfair treatment in Kuwait by the Sunni majority. This led to the government introducing more discriminatory measures against them, alienating loyal Shi'ites. During the Iraqi occupation, many Shi'ites remained in Kuwait, because they felt unwelcome in Saudi Arabia, a conservative Sunni society. They are regarded with suspicion by the government.

POPULATION CHANGES

Before the 1990 Iraqi invasion, Kuwait had a population of just over two million, of which between 50% and 75% were expatriates. Around 260,000 Bedoons were living in Kuwait. (Since 1988 they have been categorized as foreign residents in the population figures.) After the invasion, over 300,000 Palestinians, many of whom were thought to have supported the Iraqi invasion, were expelled. With the expulsion of the Bedoons, the Kuwaiti population now stands at an estimated 1.95 million, with only 40% being non-Kuwaiti. The government aims to decrease its reliance on non-Kuwaitis and to increase the Kuwaiti percentage, while reducing the overall population to around 1.2 million. It is hoped that Kuwaitis can be trained to fill the gaps left by the expatriates.

TRADITIONAL CLOTHES

A good tailor is highly prized and Kuwaitis will try to keep him a secret, or if they are very wealthy, employ him to work only for the family.

In Kuwait, traditional Arab clothes are worn alongside European-style suits and dresses, casual clothes, Indian saris, and Punjabi suits. Although Kuwaitis once felt that European clothes were stylish and better than traditional wear, they now feel proud of their cultural heritage and realize that their clothes are not only attractive but practical for the weather and lifestyle.

Although special sections of the souk (market) sell ready-made, traditional clothes, often imported from the Far East, the discerning Kuwaiti will choose the material to have his or her clothes made by a tailor. Many Indian and Pakistani tailors specialize in traditional Kuwaiti clothes, which are custom-made at a low price.

WOMEN'S CLOTHES Glancing at Kuwaiti women in the street will show two types of clothing. Many professional or young women wear European clothes, but some will wear a large headscarf, called a *hejab* ("he-JAHB"), to cover their hair and neck. Other women wear black *abbaya* ("ab-BAI-yah"), a sort of cloak that covers the body and clothes in loose folds of cloth. Some women cover their faces with a black cloth, *bushiya* ("boosh-ee-YAH"), or a mask or *burqa* ("BOOR-kah"). Most Bedouin or older women cover themselves in this way.

The most common form of traditional woman's dress is the *thob* ("thohb"), a long, loose dress. These can be made in any color or fabric, and are often lavishly embroidered with jewels, sequins, and gold thread. They may be made of transparent material and worn over another dress and trousers. If Kuwaiti women wear European clothes to work or outside the house, they will almost always wear a *dara'a* ("dah-RAH-ah"), a simple form of the thob like a housecoat, once they get home. A headscarf is often worn. Many women wear European-style clothes that are made with floor-length skirts, always with long sleeves and worn with the hejab. They may wear smarter versions of the dara'a to work or outside the house.

A mix of old and new can be seen in clothing for Kuwaiti women, who wear both traditional and Western-style outfits.

Kuwaiti women take great care of their appearance and tend to wear elaborate makeup, jewelry and fancy hairstyles. Most use black eyeliner for their dark eyes, the way generations of Kuwaiti women have done before them. French perfumes waft through all the social gatherings, and most women visit beauty parlors and spend hours at beauty treatments.

Children's clothes are often European in style, although traditional clothes are worn for social gatherings.

MEN'S CLOTHES The traditional clothes still favored by Kuwaiti men are very similar to those of merchants of the 19th century. They consist of a *dishdasha* ("dish-DASH-ah"), or long robe, worn over long, white trousers, or *sirwal* ("seer-WAHL"). A scarf or *gatra* ("GAT-rah") is worn on the head, held in place by a decorative rope or *agal* ("ah-GAL"). In the summer, the dishdasha and the gatra are sparkling white, but in the winter, black, navy, beige, grey, or even blue woollen dishdashas are worn, and the white gatra may be replaced with a red and white checkered one. Loose, long coats called *bisht* ("beesht") may also be worn, usually in sober colors. A fur-lined coat, or *farwah* ("fahr-WAH"), is also worn in the winter by Bedouins, who spend cold nights out in the desert.

Most Kuwaiti men wear traditional clothes all the time, at least while in Kuwait, and all wear casual versions of traditional clothes at home. It is easy to tell the non-Kuwaiti Arabs, such as the Palestinians, as they wear European clothes to work, keeping traditional clothes for the home.

A man at a market sells worry beads, which can be made of plastic, wood, silver, ivory, or even gold.

Kuwaiti men also carry worry beads or *masabah* ("mas-AB-bah"). Rarely is a Kuwaiti man seen without a set of beads, which are rolled, spun around the fingers, or passed from hand to hand.

CHILDREN'S CLOTHES   Many Kuwaiti children are well-dressed in expensive foreign clothes. Most wear fashionable European clothes on a daily basis, and many shops sell imported designer clothes that cost more than in London or Paris.

However, local tailors make traditional clothes for children, who often dress just like their parents when they attend social gatherings. The boys will be in dishdasha and the girls will wear thobs and maybe even a miniature abbaya. All children attending state schools wear uniforms.

LIFESTYLE

IN KUWAIT the family is the accepted basis of society. At the highest levels, the government is based on family ties, and throughout all levels of society, Kuwaiti political, business, and social life continues to revolve around the most important social unit, the family. Although the Kuwaiti government has provided one of the most comprehensive social welfare programs in the world, Kuwaitis still tend to see the family as their main source of support, rather than the state. The importance of the family is enhanced by Kuwait's small size and population, which allows accessibility to political leaders through family networks, by means of the diwaniyah meetings.

Despite oil wealth, Western influences, and the trauma of the Iraqi invasion, family values remain conservative, based firmly on Islamic principles. A woman's role in the family as wife and mother, for instance, is basically unchanged despite increased education.

Kuwait is a country of very visible wealth and conspicuous consumption. All Kuwaitis like to have the newest and best of everything. They also generally have a lot of time on their hands, thanks to the short working hours. Apart from the desert, there is urban life, where everyone drives, or is driven, in their plush air-conditioned cars between air-conditioned houses, shopping malls, and offices. Although one can still see the ravages of the Iraqi occupation, Kuwait is on the whole clean and organized. Few traces of antiquity remain, and these are now carefully preserved. Kuwaitis like order, and their lifestyle is generally conservative, despite their wealth and interest in all new technology.

Above: **A coffee break at a café. Kuwaitis have a lot of free time to enjoy their wealth.**

Opposite: **This Kuwaiti woman wears an abbaya, a black cloak that covers the head and clothes.**

63

THE SOCIAL ASPECT OF THE DIWANIYAH

For the majority of Kuwaitis, social life revolves around the diwaniyah, a regular weekly meeting, generally of men who are related and their friends. Here, over coffee, they meet to discuss business, politics, arrange introductions, or grant favors. Diwaniyahs may be held at any time, but tend to be mostly in the afternoon and evening. Tea and other drinks are always served, as well as snacks like fruit and nuts. A meal may be served, especially late at night, when the guests may bring with them pots of special food. The style of a diwaniyah meeting is usually quite traditional, that is, guests remove their shoes and sit on the floor. If a meal is served, it will be spread on newspaper or a cloth, depending on the degree of formality, and the food eaten from communal dishes. Men may attend several diwaniyahs a week, although there may be hundreds of sessions taking place every night in every Kuwaiti suburb. Typically, a man will hold a diwaniyah on Saturday and Sunday evenings, and his son will host one on Thursday and Friday evenings. The other evenings may be spent at other diwaniyahs or with close relatives.

Kuwaiti law is largely based on Islamic law, which treats men and women quite differently. Women need the permission of a male guardian to marry, and a woman's inheritance is half that of a man's.

A PLACE FOR EVERYONE WITHIN THE FAMILY

If the family is the most important unit in Kuwait, children are the focus of the family. All Kuwaitis love children, and they are included in almost all social gatherings. Even when there are servants to care for them, parents will still be fully involved in their children's lives. Most forms of entertainment are aimed at families, and there are few social activities that are restricted to adults. The concept of boarding or summer school does not exist in Kuwait. As grandparents may well be part of the family unit, children are generally surrounded by devoted relatives. Some Kuwaitis are concerned about the new generation, as children are usually overindulged and servants are reluctant to discipline them.

Children tend to be separated by gender early on, and from the time they are old enough to sit still, boys often attend the diwaniyah with their fathers. Girls stay at home or visit with their mothers, although small girls are welcomed into male gatherings, often with great delight. Children live at home until they marry, and possibly even after that, especially if the parents would otherwise be left alone. Single people never live alone, although they may have separate apartments within a family complex.

Generally in Kuwait, one's position in the family depends on gender and age. Men and older people have higher status in the family and their opinions are most highly respected. Although the government provides free care for the elderly, it is needed only in the rare cases of old people with no family. Older people live in the family as respected guardians of tradition. It would be a social embarrassment to abandon one's parents. Religious and traditional values ensure that the family provides for all its members.

KUWAITI WOMEN: MANY GAINS, BUT STILL A LONG WAY TO GO

Popular misconceptions of the role of women in the Arab Gulf states do not apply in Kuwait. Women are not enslaved in harems, shrouded in black (unless they choose to be), and denied any public role. However, men and women have different identities and interests in Kuwait, and men and women are by no means entirely equal. The family is the center of social life, and women's roles within the family are primarily as wives and mothers. The majority of women marry and usually remarry if they are divorced or widowed. The few unmarried women live with their families.

Women volunteers helping out handicapped children. Kuwaiti women are now better educated, with women making up the majority of students at Kuwait University.

The government supports equality between the sexes in several areas. Women have ready access to housing, health care, and education. Although the literacy rate for women is lower than that for men, the situation is improving. In 1960 the first group of Kuwaiti women was sent to study at Cairo University in Egypt. After the opening of Kuwait University in 1966, women soon made up the majority of students (over 60%). Of those majoring in science, 70% are women, although they make up only 34% in law and 38% in engineering and petroleum. Still, this compares favorably with the number of women in American universities.

WOMEN AT WORK

Despite the number of women graduates, many of them are unlikely to work. In 1985 only 13.8% of Kuwaiti women over the age of 15 worked, a significant increase from 1975, when only 6% worked. One-third of working women are teachers, while the others work primarily in the social services and clerical positions, although some are active in the business world. Most of the working women are foreigners. The reason for the low number of working women lies partly within society's attitude toward work, for both men and women.

In Kuwait, fewer people than in any other country need to work for a salary. Only 59% of Kuwaiti men work because so many of them have other income. Some older Kuwaitis object to women working, especially when this means they would have to come in contact with men. As women live with their families, they must respect the decision of the head of the household.

Many Kuwaiti men do not have to work and women are not encouraged to do so, despite favorable working conditions, even for those with children.

Kuwaitis entertain a great deal, have servants to supervise, and high standards of housework to meet. There are no state nurseries, and in the past foreign nannies were employed. This became a controversial issue and there was even a campaign against the influence of foreign nannies on children. Now, women have up to two years of maternity leave at half pay. The working day for state employees is short, usually ending at 1 p.m. Employers are usually understanding about women needing time off to care for sick children. So working conditions for Kuwaiti women are very favorable, allowing them to be home in time for lunch with their children. Nevertheless, it appears that just as most Kuwaiti men are ambivalent about work, women are even more so.

WOMEN'S DRESS: A PRIVATE CHOICE?

The Islamic way of dressing for women was, until recently, considered a matter for private choice in Kuwait. But lately this has become more of a public issue, particularly at the university. The Islamicist opposition wants Islamic dress made compulsory, but others want it banned from the university and public offices. During the war some Kuwaitis were influenced by contact with the conservative Saudi Arabians or with Westerners. Their experiences resulted in various views about women, particularly about their clothes.

Women wearing face masks have been officially banned from driving for safety reasons, but they can still be seen behind the wheel. Some women feel that the Islamicist groups offer the only opposition to the government and show their support by wearing traditional clothes. Women who were brave enough to wear European clothes in the past now feel they should wear them with long hemlines, or they now opt for traditional clothes.

A well-covered female shopper. There are many degrees of Islamic or traditional clothing, and women are often under pressure from several directions in the choice of their attire.

67

A family enjoys a day out together at an amusement center. Kuwaiti children are doted upon and usually enjoy huge material benefits.

BIRTH

The birth of a child is always a source of great delight and celebration, even more so if the child is a boy. The government gives all parents a cash gift for each baby born, and it continues to pay a monthly allowance of 50 Kuwaiti dinars (approximately US$165) until the child marries or gets a job. In modern Kuwait, women give birth usually in a hospital rather than at home as in the past. The baby will often be swaddled or wrapped tightly in cloth and will be named when seven days old. Boys are always circumcised, and this is usually done in the hospital at a very young age.

MARRIAGE

Most Kuwaitis marry as this is considered the norm and the most socially acceptable situation for all adults. The men marry in their mid-20s and women in their early 20s. Mothers assume the responsibility of finding marriage partners. Kuwaitis usually marry within the family.

MARRIAGE IN ISLAM

Men can marry Christian and Jewish women, although it is not encouraged, and they do not need permission from their parents to marry. Women can marry only Muslim men, and they usually need permission from their male guardian to wed. Men can have up to four wives at a time, provided he can treat them all equally. Women can marry only one man at a time. A man can divorce a woman by stating "I divorce you" three times. He must then pay her a sum agreed in the marriage contract so she can live without him. A woman can only divorce her husband if he does not provide for her. After divorce, children remain in their father's custody.

THE WEDDING PARTY

Within a few months, or a year at most, of the engagement, two wedding parties are held, one for the bride's family and one for the groom's. The groom will wear traditional clothes, and the bride will wear a European wedding dress. Dancing (with partners of the same sex) will celebrate the occasion, which will go on for many hours, with soft drinks, tea, and probably a meal. All Kuwaiti families spend as much money as possible on weddings, and this is an important source of social prestige. Hundreds or even thousands of guests may be invited. The government gives all new grooms US$13,000, half of this as a loan, to finance some of the festivities.

Once a marriage is likely, the parents will finalize the details. These include an agreed amount of gold jewelry to be given to the woman by the man's family and possibly some money. The total cost may be as much as US$50,000. The official marriage may take place quietly, but will only be considered an engagement. The couple may be alone with each other, but do not live together. When they do, a big party will mark this stage.

DIVORCE

In the past, divorce rates were very low in Kuwait, thanks to the support of the extended family and also because most women were financially dependent. There was also great social shame attached to being divorced, and a woman would generally lose her children to her husband's family. The gradual breakdown of the extended family, greater women's education and job opportunities, and increasing outside influences, especially during the 1990 Gulf War, all seem to have contributed to an increase in the divorce rate. Over one-third of marriages where both partners are Kuwaiti currently end in divorce.

A Kuwaiti father spends time with his family. Sourcing marriage and business partners from among relatives is always preferred, as a failed marriage can be concealed within the family, reducing loss of face.

SAVING FACE

The concept of face in Kuwait has the same meaning as respect and reputation in the West, but there is an intensity about it that is almost inconceivable to a Westerner. A Kuwaiti spends his life building and maintaining face, and the amount of face that he earns is an indication of the degree to which he serves and protects the family's interests.

Children learn about saving face from early childhood. A child is considered to be an adult when he realizes that his own success, or face, is directly related to that of his family's. Every adult's face is affected by the behavior of his or her relatives. This sense of face lies behind most behavior in social and business settings. Although becoming rich can add face, visible failure in business loses it, which is why many hold on to unsuccessful businesses.

DEATH

As for all Muslims, Kuwaitis are buried within 24 hours of death. The body is washed, wrapped in white cloth, and carried by men to the grave, where it is buried without a coffin, facing Mecca. There are usually no flowers, and the grave is marked simply with a small plinth or paving slab. Male mourners do not shave, and women wear black. A memorial service may be held at a mosque. Guests express their condolences over the next 40 days, keeping the bereaved family company.

HEALTH CARE

Kuwait is divided into six health regions, each with a government-run general hospital. There are several specialist hospitals. In total, 17 hospitals serve Kuwait's needs, providing 6,000 beds, or one per 357 people. Primary health care is provided by the state through a network of polyclinics. Medications prescribed by a doctor are free at hospitals or in government pharmacies. Dental care is also free and there are 160 dental clinics.

Over 12,000 health professionals practice in Kuwait, including 2,500 doctors and 7,000 nurses, mostly expatriate workers. Any patient with needs not met in Kuwait will be sent abroad at government expense. A small private sector employs 300 doctors and 700 nurses in a few clinics in Kuwait City.

The government has also established a clinic for the care of those who were injured, physically or psychologically, at the hands of the Iraqi invaders. The clinic offers practical and mental support to people who were tortured or traumatized by the invasion.

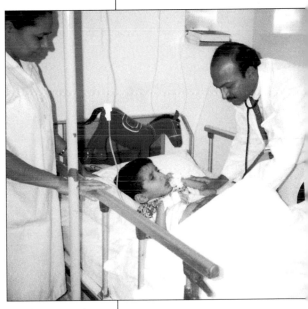

Kuwait's cradle-to-grave health care has been a success in several respects. Kuwaiti men have a life expectancy of 74, women 78, which is comparable with the figures for the United States.

Universal education in Kuwait has raised the literacy level from 5% at independence in 1961 to the present level of nearly 80%.

EDUCATION

Until the 1930s, education in Kuwait was entirely private, consisting of Koranic schools. Since 1965 there has been free education from kindergarten to graduate school. One-third of state employees are connected to this enormous education system. There are almost 100 private schools. These are only for expatriate workers but come under state supervision. Many teachers are foreigners; in the 1980s, over 70% were non-Kuwaiti Arabs. The government is trying to remedy this situation by training more Kuwaitis and encouraging more women to enter the profession.

Kindergarten is available for all 4-year-olds, and education is compulsory from 6 to 14. Children under 16 are forbidden to work, so almost all Kuwaitis attend school until they are at least 16 years old. After kindergarten, boys and girls attend separate schools, although university education is coeducational. Classes are small, rarely with more than 20 students in a class. The school day starts early at 7:15 a.m. and finishes at 1 p.m. All schoolchildren wear uniforms and there is no school on Thursday and

Friday, the Kuwaiti weekend. There is a three-month holiday in the summer and short holidays for major festivals. In 1991–92, two school years were compressed into one, and there were classes in the afternoons to make up for the lessons missed because of the Iraqi invasion. Children study English starting in the fifth grade. Extracurricular activities are not as important to Kuwaiti children as to American children, and physical exercise is not part of the curriculum, although the government provides sport clubs and recreation centers.

Kuwait University, which was set up in 1966, has more than 17,000 students, with 9,500 women and 5,000 non-Kuwaitis. The faculty consists of 900 professors and associate professors; 300 of them are Kuwaiti citizens. The university offers degrees in arts, sciences, education, commerce, law, engineering, Islamic studies, medicine, and health sciences. All the science and engineering courses are taught in English, but the arts, humanities, and social sciences are in Arabic. Most students who wish to do postgraduate studies are sent abroad at government expense.

Schoolchildren spend the day at the zoo. An estimated 400,000 students attend 600 state schools in Kuwait, costing the government approximately US$4,000 per student each year.

An old gate reflects the more traditional architecture of Kuwait City's early buildings.

TRADITIONAL KUWAITI HOUSES

Traditionally, Kuwaiti houses, like many in the Middle East, presented a forbidding front to the world. In the old city, rows of blank, plastered walls gave no hint of the houses behind the wooden doors that appeared at intervals. These carved and decorated teak doors, with carved posts and lintels, were common around the Gulf, but Kuwaiti doors had distinctive carvings of rosettes.

The plain exterior of houses had both a practical and a social purpose. Because of the hot climate, it was more practical to live in thick-walled rooms, shaded beneath columned arcades around an open courtyard, rather than in enclosed spaces. Also, the concealed courtyard offered privacy to the women; with no windows they could be totally secluded. Humble exteriors also concealed the possible wealth of the family from jealous eyes.

Traditional houses have an outer area, sometimes with a courtyard and sleeping rooms where male guests can be entertained. For the women, there is a smaller and separate inner area, ideally with its own entrance. A staircase leads to the roof, where the family sleeps when the weather is hot. Although air-conditioning means that there is no longer any need for cool courtyards or verandahs nor any reason to sleep outside, the separation of public and family quarters remains.

As Kuwaiti houses are made largely of mud, repairs are needed every year after the spring rains. But instead of repairs, the houses are often rebuilt. After the oil boom, many Kuwaitis did not carry out repairs, and houses were demolished or neglected. Modern houses are now preferred.

THE VILLA

Although some Kuwaitis and almost all expatriate workers live in apartment blocks, most Kuwaitis live in the suburbs of the cities in large houses known as villas. These villas can be built in almost any style, including Spanish hacienda and Alpine chalet. Almost all villas are white or grey, and share certain features. They all have rooftop water tanks and a series of television antennas or satellite dishes. The flat roofs are often surrounded by a wall for added privacy. They are usually square, two to three stories, designed in stone or concrete, and are decorated with marble facing, decorative windows, and elaborate façades.

Most are surrounded by a high wall with security gates, and many appear quite ordinary on the outside, a continuation of traditional architecture. The windows are usually shuttered against the heat. Inside the high walls, separate buildings may exist for branches of the family or for the servants. The interiors of houses are spacious, with large reception rooms and high ceilings.

Modern Kuwaiti houses are often luxurious, with crystal light fittings, marble and imported stone floors, and elaborate furnishings.

RELIGION

THE VAST MAJORITY OF KUWAITIS are Muslims, as the followers of Islam are called, and their Muslim identity is as important, or even more so, than being Kuwaiti or Arab. To Muslims, Islam is much more than a set of beliefs. It offers a complete guide to every aspect of life and influences their daily behavior. Five pillars or requirements form the basis of Islam: profession of faith, praying five times daily, giving alms, fasting during the Islamic month of Ramadan, and making a pilgrimage to Mecca. The five pillars, as well as obligations such as being honest and just, a willingness to defend Islam, and prohibitions such as not eating pork, drinking alcohol, or lending money for interest or gambling, form common bonds among Muslims.

Kuwait lies on the Arabian Peninsula, the birthplace of the Prophet Mohammed and of Islam, the religion he founded. Islam means "to submit" in Arabic. A Muslim submits to the will of God, which was revealed through prophets, including those recognized by Judaism and Christianity. For Muslims, the last of these prophets was Mohammed, to whom the Koran, the word of God, was revealed by the Angel Gabriel, in the seventh century of the Christian era.

Prophet Mohammed established a new religion when he founded the first Muslim community in Medina, now in Saudi Arabia, in 622. The Islamic calendar starts at this point, so like all Islamic countries, Kuwait operates with two calendars. Although the Prophet died 10 years later, his followers established a vast empire until all of the Middle East, North Africa, and parts of Europe were united in the Muslim faith.

Above: **A modern mosque not only serves as a place of worship but also as a place for religious instruction.**

Opposite: **A child learns how to say her prayers, which are always in Arabic and performed five times a day.**

Although there are many mosques in Kuwait, the daily prayers can be performed anywhere.

PRAYER AND IMPORTANCE OF TIME

The most important daily aspect of Islam to most Muslims is the second pillar, the requirement to pray five times a day. The prayers, which are said in Arabic, are directed toward Mecca. Before praying, Muslims must wash their face, arms, head, and feet in a prescribed manner. They must also be ritually clean, in that they should wash thoroughly after certain activities, such as using the toilet. Women are excused from praying when they are menstruating or have recently given birth.

Although prayers can be performed up to an hour each side of the set times, it is considered better to pray on time. Prayers can be offered almost anywhere, even in the street, but many men, and some women, prefer to pray in a mosque. Prayer times are announced from loudspeakers on the minarets of the many mosques, and most people will stop work to pray. All public places, such as airports or shopping malls, provide a place to pray. In case the direction of Mecca is not indicated, many Kuwaitis carry

THE FIVE PILLARS OF ISLAM

1.	shahada ("sha-ha-DAH")	Professing faith—that there is no God but Allah, and Mohammed is his prophet—in the form of a recitation in Arabic, makes one a Muslim.
2.	salat ("sal-AT")	Praying five times a day in the correct manner.
3.	zakat ("za-KAAT")	Giving alms to the needy or to good causes.
4.	saum ("sowm")	Fasting (not even water) between sunrise and sunset for the 28 days of the Islamic month of Ramadan.
5.	haj ("haaj")	Making the pilgrimage to Mecca at least once in a lifetime.

a small compass. Adult men try to attend the midday prayers at a mosque on Fridays, the Muslim holy day. This is not just a time for prayer but also a social occasion and a chance to attend a lecture by a religious figure.

THE GLORIOUS KORAN

Prophet Mohammed was not the author of the Koran, but its messenger. The Koran is for Muslims the final word of God, replacing and correcting the Old and New Testaments, and any other holy books. During Prophet Mohammed's lifetime, the Koran was memorized in parts, but after his death it was all written down, and it remains unchanged. It is arranged in 114 named chapters, divided into 6,236 verses. It has no clear beginning or end, rather all parts are interconnected by rhyme, rhythm, and meaning. Not a single dot or letter can be changed without altering the entire text. All Muslims study the Koran, and children in Kuwaiti schools memorize all or parts of it, and study its meaning and interpretation.

Thousands of Muslims congregate in Mecca every year for the pilgrimage, which brings together Muslims from all over the world.

THE PILGRIMAGE: THE AIM OF A LIFETIME

All Muslims aim to make the pilgrimage or haj to Mecca at least once in a lifetime. Kuwaitis are fortunate in that they live so close to Mecca, which is in Saudi Arabia, on the other side of the Arabian Peninsula. Muslims who make the pilgrimage have the honor of adding the title Haji ("ha-JEE") for a man, or Hajieh ("ha-JEE-eh") for a woman, before their names.

The pilgrimage is undertaken at a certain time of the year and visits outside this period do not count as the real pilgrimage. All business must be set in order before departure, a leftover from the time that the journey would take months, if not years. Throughout the pilgrimage, pilgrims must not use soap or perfume, cut their hair or nails, or damage anything in nature, and men and women must not sleep together. All men wear two white, seamless sheets of cloth, and women keep their faces unveiled.

The rituals of the pilgrimage last nine days, and two million people perform the same ritualistic actions that commemorate certain incidents in

A PROPHET AND A MODEL FOR MUSLIMS

The life of Prophet Mohammed is considered to be a model for all Muslims. Much of what he said and did was recorded by writers, and these traditions, together with the Koran, are used by Muslims as a guide to living.

Born in A.D. 570, he was a poor orphan who later worked as a trader. When he was 25 he married his employer, a rich widow of 40 called Khadijah, who became the first Muslim. After she died, leaving him with a daughter, Fatima, he did not remarry for many years until his role as a leader of the Muslims led him to do so a few times for a variety of reasons. He left no adult sons. Many Muslims claim to be descendants of his family. They call themselves Sayyeds ("say-YEDS"), and are honored by other Muslims.

Although he became wealthy, Prophet Mohammed led a simple life and was famed for his kindness to his family and friends, as well as to anyone who approached him for help. Although Muslims are proud of the way he led his life and of his achievements, they are careful to distinguish this from any notion that they follow him, instead of God and Islam.

the lives of the prophets. The pilgrimage climaxes with the slaughter of an animal, which is then given to the poor, and the male pilgrim shaves his head. Many Muslims then visit the town of Medina, where Prophet Mohammed is buried.

THE SHI'ITES

The majority of Kuwaitis are Sunni Muslims, but there is a significant minority of Shi'ites (10–25% of the population). The Shi'ites broke away from the majority of Muslims soon after the death of Prophet Mohammed over the question of who should be leader. The Shi'ites felt that Ali, the prophet's son-in-law, and his descendants should be chosen as leaders.

Today, Shi'ites are a majority only in Iran. Sunni and Shi'ite Muslims all follow the basic five pillars of Islam, but differ on the interpretation of Islamic teachings, tend not to intermarry, and pray in different mosques. The Shi'ites have their own calendar of religious festivals; these are related to events in the lives of the people they believe should have inherited the leadership of Islam.

Many of the stories from the Old and New Testaments appear in the Koran, often in a slightly different form. For example, in the story of Abraham's testing by God, it is his son Ismael, and not Isaac, whom Abraham is ready to sacrifice at God's demand. The only woman's name in the Koran is that of Mary (Maryam in Arabic), the mother of Jesus (Esau), who is revered as a prophet. These and many of the names in the Koran are quite familiar to Christians in their Anglicized forms.

A Roman Catholic church in Kuwait. Members of Kuwait's large expatriate community are free to practice their own faiths.

NON-MUSLIM RELIGIOUS MINORITIES

Kuwait has a small Arab Christian community, the result of missionary activity in the early 20th century, as well as many resident foreign Christians from Europe, India, and the Far East. Some Kuwaiti Jewish trading families have lived in Kuwait for a long time, although now very few remain.

The Kuwait constitution guarantees freedom of belief and worship, but bans attempts to convert Muslims to other religions. There are several churches in Kuwait, including a Catholic cathedral. However, certain activities contrary to Islam are forbidden in Kuwait, such as drinking alcohol, using drugs, and insulting religious figures or beliefs.

SUPERSTITION

Traditionally, Bedouin Arabs, as well as practicing Muslims, were very superstitious. Some traditional beliefs remain in evidence today in Kuwaiti

ISLAMIC OVERSEAS AID

One way in which Kuwait combines its Islamic identity with its successful oil economy is in its overseas aid program. Donating to the needy is one of the pillars of Islam and one which the Kuwaiti government has been practicing for the last 35 years. Initially, aid was directed at Arab countries, but after 1974, the Kuwait Fund For Arab Economic Development extended its scope, with aid projects for 13 needy countries around the world.

Approximately 4% of Kuwait's Gross Domestic Product goes to low interest loans or donations to needy countries, considerably more than the 0.7% suggested by the United Nations. The United States and Japan are the largest world aid donors, but their contributions represent less than 0.3% of their respective GDPs. Kuwait provides around US$500 million a year in aid, one quarter of the overseas aid provided by the entire Arab world. Most of the money is invested in large-scale civil engineering projects, such as building dams and water supply facilities.

There are no ministers in Islam, as understood by Christians, and there is no organized clergy as such. Imams ("im-AHMS") provide religious teaching, lead prayers and certain religious rites, and run the mosques. They are not essential for any of these services, which can be performed by any adult male Muslim.

society, as in much of the Middle East. One of the most common beliefs is the need to guard against the evil eye. This is a curse that arises when someone is jealous, or that comes from someone who unfortunately possesses the evil eye, even if they are unaware of their power. Just a glance from one of these people can bring extreme bad luck.

Guarding against the evil eye takes two main forms. First, no one should boast about his or her good fortune or wealth, and if anything positive is said, the speaker should remember to thank God for this good luck. For this reason, some people do not point out another's good fortune, in case they are thought to be jealous.

The second main weapon against the evil eye is the use of charms and amulets. The amulets are often shaped like hands or eyes and blue stones are used for decoration. Gold jewelry often uses these designs. Charms can be used to decorate animals, clothes, tents, and houses. Charms are used especially to guard children from the evil eye.

The written words of the Koran are equally useful as protection and can be written on paper or metal. Even today, there are few Kuwaiti children who do not wear a gold charm with such writings around their neck or pinned to their clothes.

THE MOSQUE

There are mosques in most public buildings in Kuwait and in such places as airports, offices, and shopping malls. The most obvious external feature is the minaret, from where the calls for prayer are announced. An indispensable feature is a place where worshipers can wash before praying. A mosque has no furniture, but it is well carpeted so that the worshipers can kneel, sit, and stand in comfort while praying. There is usually a pulpit, so that a prayer leader can give a sermon after leading the prayers.

The mosque is clearly oriented in the direction of Mecca. The symbol of Islam, a crescent and star, usually decorates the dome. Mosques are also often used as places for teaching, meeting, and quiet meditation.

In Kuwait women have special rooms or galleries in many mosques so that they will not be seen by men. Non-Muslims can visit mosques, as long as they are People of the Book, that is, Jews and Christians. While in a mosque, they must observe the same rules as Muslims. They must remove their shoes to ensure the floor remains clean and wear clothes that cover their arms and legs. Women must cover their hair, and men are encouraged to wear a hat or headcovering.

Muslim prayer times:
salat ul fajr *(dawn or sunrise);* salat ul zuhr *(midday);* salat ul asr *(mid-afternoon);* salat al maghrib *(sunset); and* salat al isha *(90 minutes after sunset).*

THE GRAND MOSQUE

There are more than 770 mosques in Kuwait, from simple neighborhood ones with space for a maximum of 1,000 worshipers to grand buildings that can accommodate many thousands of people. Over 200 mosques in Kuwait remain closed because of the considerable damage inflicted on them during the Iraqi occupation. One mosque that has been fully restored and which Kuwaitis are very proud of is the Grand Mosque.

Opened in 1986 and built at a cost of 13 million Kuwaiti dinars (US$43 million), it lays claim to being the world's most innovative mosque. It covers 484,376 square feet (45,000 square meters), and can accommodate 5,000 male and 550 female worshipers. It has places for 106 people to perform their ritual ablutions at a time, and parking space for 500 cars.

Its architecture uses various traditional Islamic styles and the building was constructed using modern technology, combining reinforced concrete, natural stone, and decorative marble.

The Grand Mosque provides not only a place of worship, but a massive library and reading hall, as well as a conference center and a reception hall for VIPs.

Opposite: **Calls to prayer can be heard from the minarets of mosques. When traveling, Kuwaitis carry alarm clocks or wear special watches with built-in compasses that indicate the prayer times and the direction of Mecca.**

LANGUAGE

ARABIC IS THE NATIVE LANGUAGE of about 70% of Kuwait's population and the sacred language of all Muslims, who are 80% of Kuwait's population. It is the official language of Kuwait, and all government documents and notices are in modern standard Arabic.

English, particularly American English, is the second language for most educated Kuwaitis. It is important in business circles, but getting around with just English could be difficult, although street and many shop signs are in both English and Arabic.

Many other languages are spoken in Kuwait, reflecting the diverse origins of the many expatriates in the country. In particular, Farsi (Persian), Hindi, and Punjabi are widely heard in the streets and souks (markets).

Arabic is spoken by over 200 million people in the world and is the official language of 17 countries. It is an important link between Kuwaitis and the rest of the Middle East and North Africa. Three main forms of Arabic exist: classical, the language of the Koran; modern standard, which is used for writing in all countries and for communication between Arabs from different regions; and colloquial or spoken Arabic.

Each Arabic region has its own dialect: that of Kuwait is a mixture of Bedouin dialects and the dialect of the Gulf traders. It is liberally mixed with Persian, Indian, Egyptian, and American words that have been borrowed, making it sound distinctly different from other Arabic dialects. Its sounds are a little softer and less glottal (the sound that is made in the back of the throat). This dialect is considered by Gulf Arabs to be somewhat new and hip, in keeping with the image of Kuwait as being a very modern country.

Above: **A typical Kuwaiti license plate.**

Opposite: **A shop attracts customers with signs in both English and Arabic.**

ARABIC—THE LANGUAGE OF GOD

Arabic is more than a mother tongue to Kuwaitis. For all Muslims, it is the sacred language in which the Koran was revealed by God to Prophet Mohammed. *Koran* means recitation in Arabic. For many Muslims, the Koran should not be translated into other languages, but read only in Arabic, as it is perfect in its original form. A Muslim prays in Arabic, whatever his or her mother tongue, and all Muslims aim to be able to read and recite the Koran in Arabic. Arabic is possibly the main cultural link between the world's one billion Muslims, of whom only one-sixth are Arabs. Many common Arabic expressions are derived from the Muslim faith and are used throughout the Muslim world. Examples of common expressions include:

A teacher at an evening Koranic class. Arabic is a phonetic-based language that has fewer letters than English.

as-salaamu alaykum	peace be upon you (used as a greeting)
wa-alaykum salaam	and peace be upon you too (standard reply)
alhamdillalah	thanks be to God (used whenever good news is given)
bismillah	in the name of God (used before eating or undertaking many activities)
insha'allah	God willing (used after every statement concerning the future)
mashallah	blessings of God (used whenever something is positive)
ya allah	hurry, with God's help
wa allah	by God, truthfully

Many Kuwaitis like to decorate their homes, offices, and cars with these expressions, or verses taken from the Koran. These are written in beautifully flowing calligraphy.

LEARNING ARABIC

Arabic has 10 sounds that do not exist in English, although some of these sounds are used in other languages such as Spanish. Arabic grammar is complex, but it has some similarities with Greek and Latin. All nouns are either male or female, and the form of the noun differs according to whether you are referring to one, two, or more of that item. Thus, it can be hard to identify a word, unless you know all three versions, which can be very different.

Arabic script is written from right to left and is entirely phonetic, that is, it is written exactly as it sounds. The writing is always joined fluidly, and there are no capital letters. Each letter has up to three forms, depending on whether it appears at the beginning, in the middle, or at the end of a word. There are, however, fewer letters than in the English alphabet. Not all vowels are written, as there are fewer sounds than in English, but little marks can indicate the vowel sounds for beginners or in foreign words.

Possibly the most commonly used polite expression in Kuwait is ahlan wa sahlan *or "at home and at ease," used roughly to mean "welcome." This was originally used by Bedouins to greet travelers, but is now used by hosts, business people, and tradesmen, to mean "relax, be comfortable."*

A Kuwaiti child must be named so that his parentage and clan are apparent.

YOU ARE WHAT YOU ARE CALLED

Kuwaitis' names are clues to their ancestry. Kuwaitis have a profound sense of their heritage, and many can trace their ancestors to the clans who arrived with the Bani Utub. A few can trace their origins to clans that already lived in the area. Some prominent families arrived later from other Gulf states, and those of Persian origin arrived mostly during the late 19th and early 20th century. Kuwaiti names tell us a great deal about the person. They indicate his or her parentage, clan, or ethnic origin, and so his or her social importance.

The names of a Kuwaiti man or woman will always follow a set order: a given name, father's name, and then the surname—for example, Mohammed Abdullah al-Shayah is Mohammed, son of Abdullah, of the Shayah family. The name of a grandfather may be inserted after the father's name, for example Mohammed Abdullah al-Jabir al-Shayah's grandfather's name is Jabir. Generally speaking, the more important the person, the longer the name. The surname is always that of a common ancestor, and all persons with that name will be related, however distantly.

An exception is Kuwaitis of Iranian origin, whose surname may indicate their approximate place of origin, for example the surname Behbani means the person's ancestors belong to the village of Behban.

Women's given names differ, but they will also use their family and father's names. They do not change their names when they marry, as they will always belong to the same tribe and father all their lives. As marriages between cousins are common, many couples do share the same surname, but the father's name will, of course, be different.

ARABIC NAMES

Almost all Kuwaitis have Arabic first names, often the name of their parents or grandparents, and most names have religious connotations. These include the names of the prophets or saints, like Mohammed, Yusef (Joseph), Musa (Moses), and names of devotion to God, like Abdullah (slave of God) and Abdul Rahman (slave of the merciful one). Other names indicate good qualities, like Mubarak (good fortune), and Salem (good health). Great thought is given to choosing names, often with the help of the Koran, and they can reflect events at the time of birth or the parents' hopes for their child. Many men's names have a feminine version, usually by adding the female ending, eh/yeh—for example Amir for a man, Amireh for a woman. So women may have names with similar meanings to men. They can also be named after female religious figures, such as Maryam (Mary), Aisha, and Khadijah (the wives of Prophet Mohammed). Additionally, many women's names have lovely meanings, such as Jamileh (beautiful, where the male version is Jamil), Sultana (queen), and Yasmina (jasmine).

NAMES WITHIN THE FAMILY In most respects, Kuwaiti names follow the general Arab conventions. It is an essential part of Arabic and Islamic culture to honor one's parents, and no one can change or give up his or her father's name. For this reason, adoption is frowned on, as a child must always use his or her father's name. People may be referred to as son (ibn) or daughter (bint) of someone when they are introduced for the first time, for example, Mohammed ibn Abdullah.

Another custom within the family and among friends is to refer to people as mother (umm) or father (abu) of their eldest son. Thus Abdullah and his wife, Khadijah, once their son Mohammed is born, may be thereafter referred to as Abu Mohammed and Umm Mohammed. This indicates the pride that Arabs have in their children, especially the firstborn son. Although it is possible to be called after a girl child, this is very unusual and only done if there are no sons in the marriage. Many husbands and wives refer to each other in this way, as it is considered more suitable for married people. The family, and one's place within it, is really the key to people's names in Kuwait.

A name in neon lights. A Kuwaiti name reflects both the Arabic and Islamic heritage.

Men are demonstrative to each other in public but face and honor must be maintained at all times.

POLITE RITUALS

Arabic has many expressions that are part of polite formalities. An acquaintance is greeted enthusiastically, and lengthy enquiries will be made after his or her health and that of the family or any mutual friends. This may last for several minutes. A man will not usually refer to another man's wife unless they are related, but he may ask after the family in general. It is very rude to rush straight to business without the proper formalities. Generally before business of any sort, tea or coffee will be offered. Kuwaitis are very polite and sociable, and this extends to all areas of life, not just social activities.

Kuwaitis are so polite that the word "no" is rarely used, so as not to cause disappointment. Things are usually *insha'allah* or "as God wills." This is part of the general Kuwaiti culture of avoiding unpleasantness. Kuwaitis tend to conceal their anger in public; it would be a serious loss of face for a person to show any lack of personal control. Kuwaitis show their displeasure in subtle ways, by slight gestures or by a faint lack of enthusiasm. These are all easily detected by other Kuwaitis.

Kuwaitis are generally very concerned about their honor or social face. This means that they behave in a generally dignified manner at all times. Adult men walk with dignity, sit up straight when in company, and pay great attention to their appearance. Kuwaiti men and women do not touch each other in public. However, it is common to see women showing great affection to each other in public, while men kiss and hug each other in greeting. Men do not kiss women to whom they are not related. Women do not generally shake hands with men.

THE MEDIA

The media is mostly state-owned, although some private newspapers are run under the supervision of the Ministry of Communications. Historically, the press was free to report on most matters, but after 1986 many restrictions were introduced, and many foreign reporters were expelled. Many newspapers were run by Palestinians, and so their expulsion left a gap that led to the lack of any really dynamic newspapers.

A board provides information in Arabic on seatbelt safety.

There are five daily newspapers in Arabic and two in English—*The Arab Times* and *The Kuwait Times*. There are also newspapers in Hindi and Urdu. Over 70 magazines are published in Kuwait. Newspapers are not cheap, around 150 fils (50 US cents), but slightly more people in Kuwait read newspapers than in the United States. (244 newspapers sold per 1,000 people in Kuwait, compared to 238 in the United States). This reflects the interest that Kuwaitis have in the rest of the world. The editor of one of the major daily newspapers, *al-Watan*, is a woman.

Although there are four Kuwaiti television channels, including one sports channel and one with English and French programs, most people have satellite dishes and so receive television programs from all over the world. Television channels that show Egyptian films and programs are very popular.

There are no private radio stations in Kuwait, but the state channels broadcast all types of music—Arabic and foreign, old and modern. Every evening a channel broadcasts news and programs in English, and the American Armed Forces Radio broadcasts from Doha, to the north of Kuwait City.

Foreign newspapers and magazines are censored, and articles that are considered unsuitable, as well as photographs of scantily-clad women, are blacked out with a felt-tipped pen.

ARTS

KUWAIT HAS A National Council for Culture, Arts, and Letters, founded in 1974, that is responsible for culture, fine arts, the national heritage, and public libraries. The government is dedicated to developing all aspects of Kuwaiti arts and a great deal is invested on rediscovering lost art forms and encouraging new ones. Many traditional arts were derived from craft activities, but many are no longer practiced.

As Kuwait is a deeply Islamic country, both its traditional and modern art forms are profoundly influenced by its religious heritage. Particularly in the past, to paint or show human figures was not allowed, as these might be used for pagan worship. This meant that abstract art or ways to praise God reflected the highest forms of Islamic art. In the performing arts, it is considered inappropriate for men to listen to women sing or watch them dance. The majority of musicians are men, and dancing, apart from performances by folkloric troupes, tends to be a single-sex activity.

Opposite: **A singing group performs a traditional song.**

Left: **Girls at a weaving class. Attempts are being made to revive some of the dying art forms.**

95

Above: **A Bedouin dance troupe. There is strong government support to keep the traditional art forms alive.**

Opposite: **A gold souk with a wide array of jewelry in the latest designs.**

BEDOUIN ARTS

Bedouin art is the most prominent expression of Kuwaiti folk art. The best examples are the textiles woven from sheep's wool; these are called *sadu* ("sa-DOO"). Wool is hand-dyed and spun and then woven into geometric designs on a portable loom. Traditionally, Bedouin women wove black tents of camel hair with decorative sadu side flaps, cushions, and saddle bags for camels. As most Bedouins now live in housing settlements, there are few women learning this craft. Eight years ago, al-Sadu House was established to keep this dying art alive, and Bedouin women are employed to demonstrate the craft.

Another Bedouin art form is the Ardah dance, which combines the agile manipulation of a sword to the accompaniment of drums, tambourines, and poetic songs. Folkloric dance troupes are supported by the government and appear regularly on television and at social occasions such as weddings. The Kuwaiti Television Folklore Troupe has presented Kuwaiti Bedouin dance and folklore at many world festivals.

BEDOUIN INDUSTRY

The traditional Bedouin name for the tent was the house of hair, as both the tent and all its contents were woven by women out of camel's hair or the wool from sheep. The women wove flat rugs for the floor and cushion covers, which were stuffed with clothes and other household cloths to furnish the tent. Large woven cloths were used to cover piles of bedding, which could be used to lean on during the day, as well as to divide the tent into rooms. The women also wove saddlebags to hold their possessions between camps, as well as decorative bridles and saddles for the camels. All this was achieved with portable wooden looms and local materials. Tools were made out of gazelle's horns; few Bedouin women owned a pair of scissors.

The wool used for weaving was spun and dyed by hand. The women managed to fit these activities in between cooking and chores such as milking, as well as making clothes and caring for their children. The finished products traditionally belonged to the men, who could sell them or keep them for use.

JEWELRY

Gold jewelry has long been a vital part of Kuwaiti culture. For Bedouins, gold and silver are a portable bank balance, and women are given large quantities of jewelry when they marry, just in case they need to support themselves. Jewelry is the most common gift on special occasions such as weddings, the birth of a child, or a birthday. The designs of gold jewelry are elaborate and include both traditional and modern touches. The latest creations of famous jewelers in Paris are copied immediately in Kuwait, and it would be hard to tell these are not the real thing.

Many Indian craftsmen also work in Kuwait, and a large section of the souk, or market, is filled with passageways lined with dazzling gold displays in shop windows. Since the early days of pearling in Kuwait, its jewelers have been skilled at creating jewelry using pearls, as well as other imported gemstones.

Although Kuwait has several movie theaters, satellite television is more popular for family entertainment, and giant satellite dishes crowd roofs and balconies of many houses.

SCULPTURE

The art of sculpture was introduced in Kuwait in 1963, when a course in sculpture was offered at the Free Atelier, or state art school. Today, there is much interest in creating sculpture in Kuwait, especially since the Kuwaiti sculptor, Sami Mohammed, won a design contest to beautify Safat Square. The winning statue is a big, open shell, 29.5 feet (9 m) high with a diameter of 5 feet (1.5 m), enclosing a stainless steel pearl. The sculpture represents Kuwait's traditional links with the sea.

CALLIGRAPHY

Calligraphy, the art of beautiful writing, is one of the most developed art forms throughout the Muslim world and is equally popular in Kuwait. Islam discourages art forms showing humans or even animals. Calligraphy avoids this restriction and serves to glorify God, as verses from the Koran are the words usually chosen. The most commonly chosen verse is the

AN ARTISTS' REFUGE

The Bayt Lothan Arts and Craft Center opened in 1994. Formerly an old Kuwaiti house that belonged to the late emir, Sheikh Sabah al-Salem al-Sabah, it was restored by his daughter, Sheikha Amal Sabah al-Salem al-Sabah. The center provides artists and the public with a place to pursue and explore their interests in art.

The center also aims to preserve Kuwait's heritage. Anyone over 4 years old can attend courses in fine arts, music, handicrafts, Islamic calligraphy, drama, and photography. All the instructors are Kuwaiti. Music is the most popular area of study, especially piano, flute, violin, and *oud* ("ood"), a type of Arab guitar.

Regular exhibitions offer artwork for sale at reasonable prices, as well as inform the public about new areas of art and the humanities. Other activities include public safety education and the sponsorship of new poets and musicians.

Bismillah, which is the opening verse of every chapter of the Koran, calling upon God, the most merciful and compassionate.

Calligraphy is used both as a decoration for books and manuscripts and for buildings. It is rendered on paper, leather, stone, glass, china, pottery, ivory, and textiles. Calligraphic designs can be woven into carpets and fabric. They can be adapted to fit any shape, and can be written in various forms, from animals to stars and flowers. There are several accepted styles of calligraphy, and artists are always working to perfect them, as well as to develop new ones.

THE THEATER

The theater has also received attention from the Kuwaiti government. The Higher Institute for Theatrical Arts trains actors and performers to degree level and encourages awareness and appreciation of theater in Kuwait. The country has four theater companies that are sponsored by the government.

Water towers are necessary to ensure adequate water pressure to the taps, but they have been turned into a distinctive and elegant architectural feature of Kuwait's cities. They are often graceful, and painted and decorated in many ways.

ARCHITECTURE

Most Kuwaitis would probably feel that their largest contribution to the arts is in the world of modern architecture. In the past, all architectural undertakings in Kuwait were foreign ventures, but now the country has enough trained architects, many with experience overseas, to design its own buildings. Although architectural remnants of old Kuwait remain, and the government is keen on restoring them, Kuwait lacks the older, elaborate architecture found in many other Arab countries. Local architecture consisted of simple mud-and-stone, single-storey houses. They were designed for function rather than form, and equipped to withstand the extreme summer heat. Modern architecture in Kuwait, however, has adventurously combined the need for protection from the elements with Islamic Arab architectural and decorative styles and modern materials and construction techniques.

The skyline of Kuwait City is dominated by a famous landmark, Kuwait Towers, strategically located at the point where Kuwait juts farthest into the Gulf. The towers of this 160-foot (49 m) building have a useful function. Two of the three blue towers are water reservoirs, and the largest has an observation deck and a rotating restaurant 132 feet (40 m) above ground. It is one of three rotating restaurants in tower buildings. One of these, the Kuwait Communication Center Tower, is over 400 feet (122 m) high. Kuwaitis are proud of how the architecture reflects the needs of the people but are not entirely utilitarian.

From the 1950s, under a series of master plans, most of old Kuwait was demolished, leaving only the gates to the old city walls. A modern city was

THE KUWAIT NATIONAL MUSEUM

The Kuwait National Museum was the most important repository of the artifacts of Kuwaiti historical and cultural life. It included art galleries and displays of antiquities and handicrafts. All of the antiquities from archeological expeditions were displayed.

Part of the museum complex, the Museum of Islamic Arts, housed a priceless collection of more than 20,000 items of Islamic art, covering 12 centuries—from huge doors to carpets, rare books and manuscripts, china and jewels. However, all were taken or destroyed by the Iraqi invaders, who also demolished the buildings. Although many of the treasures have been returned, many were damaged or are still missing. The old museum buildings are beyond repair, and the entire collection lacks a permanent home.

built, divided into zones for different commercial activities and for different groups of people to settle in, surrounded by a ring of green parks. Kuwait City, as well as the other cities, became a showpiece for outstanding modern architecture, built in tandem with roads and other public utilities. Many tall water towers, which are often distinctively designed and decorated, puncture the skyline as do the futuristic, commercial tower blocks.

LEISURE

KUWAITIS HAVE ALWAYS SPENT most of their leisure time socializing with their families and close friends, who are also usually relatives. They do this mostly at home, and particularly in the diwaniyahs, or regular social meetings, which are an essential part of Kuwaiti social, political, and cultural life. Sharing food and refreshments is an integral part of most socializing in Kuwait. Kuwaitis mostly tend to spend their leisure time with relatives and friends of the same sex, although within the close family circle and among certain social groups, men and women may socialize together. Kuwaitis love to talk, on the telephone or face to face, and relationships depend on regular and frequent exchanges.

As Kuwaitis have a lot of wealth and leisure time, a thriving leisure and entertainment industry has emerged in the last few years. As with most aspects of life, the government sees to the provision of leisure activities for the people.

Left: Soccer became even more popular after the national team's success in the World Cup in 1982.

Opposite: Camel racing is a popular sport. The jockeys are small boys, often no more than 6 years old. They ride either atop the camel's hump, or in Bedouin style, behind the hump.

Soft leather hoods cover the heads of these falcons to prevent the birds from being distracted.

All major companies, ministries, and enterprises have their own sports clubs, which often own private beaches. Competitions may be arranged between the clubs.

SPORTS

The government has invested heavily in promoting sports as a healthy pursuit for young people. There are six world-class stadiums in Kuwait. Kuwait's greatest international success has been in soccer, where the national team reached the final round of the World Cup in 1982. Swimming and equestrian competitors have also achieved international success.

There are more cricket teams than all other sporting organizations combined in Kuwait. Other popular sports include squash, rugby, baseball, and fishing. Figure skating and ice hockey are popular, especially in the summer. There are several air-conditioned indoor ice rinks; the largest can seat 1,600 spectators. Windsurfing, scuba diving, water-skiing, and jet-ski racing are also popular. Speedboat racing is a modern version of the dhow races that made Kuwait famous in the region.

FALCONRY Some traditional sports grew out of the activities of the desert. For example, falconry arose from the necessity to supplement a meager diet of dates, milk, and bread, and eventually evolved into a major sport. Hunting parties used to pursue their quarry on horseback, but four-wheel drive vehicles are now used. Wild female falcons are trapped and trained for the hunting season, which begins in late fall. A trained falcon can catch up to five birds, like bustards and curlews, in a hunting session. This sport ends at sunset, when the booty is cleaned, roasted over a fire, and eaten in the desert.

CAMEL RACING Camels were important to Bedouin Arabs, as they were the main source of transport, textiles, meat, and milk. Traditionally, Bedouins would demonstrate the superiority of their camels' bloodlines in a race. Slender, long-legged breeds were bred specially for racing, and there are official race tracks, as well as desert tracks. A camel's training begins at six months, and while a male camel's career will last up to 10 years, a female's will go on for over 20. Racing camels are fed special foods, such as oats, dates, and cow's milk.

Gambling is not allowed at horse races, but generous prizes are awarded to the winners and participants.

HORSE RACING The Arabian horse is a famed racing breed and one of the most ancient of tamed horses. It has a distinctive appearance, with a short back, small head with a concave profile, large, intelligent eyes, and a tail that it carries high. Although the Arab horse is bred for racing, it is also used to lighten and improve the heavier breeds. All thoroughbred horses are descendants of Arab stallions. The Bedouins have bred Arab horses for centuries. They are always prized, and good specimens are traditional gifts between Arab leaders. Both Arab and thoroughbred racehorses compete in Kuwait.

SHOPPING: A UNIVERSAL PASTIME

Shopping is a national pastime, and almost any item can be purchased in Kuwait, except banned items like alcohol. Men are as keen as women on shopping, and shopping malls such as the Zahra complex in al-Salmiya, and the Salhiyah and al-Mutthana complexes in Kuwait City provide an American-style shopping experience. These complexes sell consumer goods; food is found largely in neighborhood supermarkets. Kuwaitis tend to go to malls for entertainment, as these have restaurants, cafés, and fountains. Shopping is often a family activity. Entire families will visit malls, perhaps combining a shopping trip with a meal at a restaurant.

The Old Souk in Kuwait City, which is actually not more than 70 years old, offers something closer to the traditional style of shopping. It consists of covered passages and open stalls, divided into sections according to the products sold, such as fish, vegetables, clothing, and household goods. Many stalls sell only one item, for example knives or olives. Tailors have shops in the souk where they make clothes.

HOTELS, PARKS, AND ENTERTAINMENT CENTERS

Much social life takes place in the country's leading hotels, such as the Hyatt, Sheraton, and Hilton, all of which have sports facilities and restaurants. Many people meet in the coffee bars or visit the exhibitions. Hotels are the most common location for lavish weddings.

Kuwaiti families like to walk or sit in parks, especially after dark when it is cooler. Starting from the Kuwait Towers and stretching nearly 15 miles (24 km) along the shore of the Gulf, is the Waterfront Project. This park combines attractive brick and concrete walkways with rest facilities, playgrounds, and food concessions. The waterfront is lighted at night, and there are many entertainment facilities for children, including a miniature train ride.

Entertainment City, which is in the middle of the desert near Doha Village, 12 miles (19 km) north of Kuwait City, is a Disneyland-style theme park. This multi-million dollar complex, however, was completely destroyed by the Iraqis. It is now being reconstructed.

Many entertainment facilities cater to the family, especially the children.

The Khiran Resort, only 12 miles (19 km) from the Saudi Arabian border, boasts 148 chalets, parks, and a boating marina. The oldest resort in Kuwait is on Faylakah Island, just minutes by hovercraft from Kuwait City.

107

FESTIVALS

THE FESTIVALS OF KUWAIT are basically those of Sunni Islam. The Islamic calendar is based on the lunar month, which is only 29 or 30 days long, so there are only 354 days, not 365 days, in a cycle of 12 Islamic months. Thus, festivals do not fall on the same date of the Western calendar each year; they move forward by around 11 days every year. It takes 32.5 years before a festival once again falls on the same date in the Western calendar. For this reason, festivals are not associated with any particular time of year, as are Christian festivals, but can fall in any season.

Kuwait observes the Western New Year's holiday as a courtesy to its foreign residents, and a National Day (February 25). Since the Iraqi invasion and Kuwait's subsequent liberation in February 1991, Liberation Day is also celebrated on February 26.

Non-Muslim expatriates living in Kuwait are free to celebrate their own festivals, as are the Shi'ites, but there is no requirement that employers grant them those days as holidays.

Above: **During the fasting month of Ramadan, many mosques and buildings are lit up by festive fairy lights.**

Opposite: **Pilgrims in Mecca. The Eid ul-Adha festival is celebrated to mark the end of the pilgrimage.**

THE ISLAMIC CALENDAR

The Islamic year begins with Prophet Mohammed's flight from Mecca to Medina in 622 A.D. The 12 months of the Islamic calendar are:

1. Muharram	4. Rabi at-tani	7. Rajab	10. Shawal
2. Safar	5. Jumadal-ula	8. Shaaban	11. Dhulkaeda
3. Rabi al-awwali	6. Jumadal-akira	9. Ramadan	12. Dhulhijja

It is traditional to break the fast with water and a few dates, the sort of food that Prophet Mohammed would have eaten, rather than eating a big meal immediately. Many people gather in mosques, where dates are served after the sunset prayers, followed by a meal for those who wish to stay. Of course many sweets are also eaten, and the bakeries are extremely busy.

THE ISLAMIC FESTIVAL CALENDAR

There are two major Islamic holidays in Kuwait. The *Eid ul-Fitr* ("eed ul-FIT-reh"), which occurs at the end of Ramadan, a month of fasting, and the *Eid ul-Adha* ("eed ul-ADHA"), or the Festival of the Sacrifice, about three months later. The start of the Islamic year is a minor holiday with little religious significance and merits only a day's holiday, whereas the Eids mean a three- or four-day holiday. Other one-day holidays include Prophet Mohammed's birthday, which falls in the third month of the Islamic year, and the Ascension of the Prophet in the seventh month, when Mohammed was taken to heaven by God to view the world.

RAMADAN, A WELCOME TEST OF ENDURANCE

The month of Ramadan commemorates the first revelation of the Koran to Prophet Mohammed. It is a time for prayer and fasting. In 1991,

FROM FASTING TO FUN FAIRS

Once the new moon is clearly sighted and Ramadan ends, the entire country is a place of fairy lights, fun fairs, and festivities. Children receive presents and new clothes to wear when the whole family visits the mosque. Everyone celebrates for three to seven days in a round of feasting and visiting. All friends and relatives must be visited, otherwise they will be very offended. Businesses, offices, and schools are closed for three days. Near the end of Ramadan, shops are extremely crowded as people scurry around buying presents and foods for the festival.

In the past, families went to the main town square to watch men perform a Bedouin war dance, in which the men carried rifles or swords and moved slowly to the beat of drums and tambourines. This has been revived recently, only the dancers are from the national performing arts organizations.

Ramadan began as Kuwait was liberated from Iraqi forces and since then it has an even deeper meaning for most Kuwaitis.

Although it is known roughly each year when Ramadan will begin, its exact start occurs as the new moon is sighted and ends with the appearance of the next new moon. This slight uncertainty adds to the excitement for Muslims, who look forward to this special time, despite its hard tests. During the 29 or 30 days of Ramadan, all Muslims must pray on two extra occasions every day, read the Koran, be particularly kind and helpful, and try to fast from dawn to sunset. This means not eating or drinking, not even water. It also means not smoking, possibly the hardest part for most Kuwaiti men. If the month falls in the winter, it is a great relief, as the day is short and the feeling of thirst is not so acute. When, however, the month moves to the scorchingly hot summer, the fast is harder to endure. Many Kuwaitis sleep a great deal during the day at this time and spend their nights eating and socializing, with many offices and businesses closing or slowing down.

The Festival of the Sacrifice was in the past the time to give thanks for the safe return of the pearling crew. Women would parade along the sea front, singing and clapping, with their most colorful dresses on poles, to welcome home their husbands.

THE RAMADAN ROUTINE

For Muslims, prayer and fasting during Ramadan give a sense of achievement and closeness to the rest of the Muslim world. Children, women who are pregnant or with small babies, the elderly, and the sick are not expected to fast. Those forced to travel are also excused, although they are expected to make up for the days missed on another occasion. Many people feel fasting is good for the health, teaching self-discipline as well as enhancing sensitivity to the suffering of the poor.

A day during the month of Ramadan begins before dawn, often in the middle of the night, when a large meal is eaten before sunrise to prepare for the fast ahead. Restaurants are closed, except those that serve only non-Muslims and travelers, such as the airport coffee shops. After a long day, the family gathers at sunset, after prayers, and breaks the fast together. Many traditional dishes are served for this meal, which can last until late in the night. The evenings are occasions for much merriment, followed by visits to relatives and friends, or trips to shops, restaurants, and parks, which stay open late during the month. The whole family often stays awake all night, only going to bed after eating the early breakfast. No wonder children look forward to the fasting month.

NIGHT TREATS FOR WOMEN AND CHILDREN

In Kuwait, maybe more than in many other Muslim countries, the women go out after the evening meal to meet in special rooms attached to mosques or to visit each other, often with the children dressed in their best clothes. There is an additional treat for children in Kuwait during Ramadan. On the 13th night of the fast children visit from house to house, singing to the youngest member of the household and collecting gifts and sweets.

THE FESTIVAL OF THE SACRIFICE

The biggest festival in Kuwait is that of Eid ul-Adha, or the Festival of the Sacrifice. This commemorates the story of Abraham, who was willing to sacrifice his son on God's orders, a story from the Old Testament familiar to Christians and Jews. God was pleased with Abraham, so he asked him instead to sacrifice a lamb. This festival coincides with the end of the major pilgrimage to Mecca, and all Muslims who can afford it sacrifice a goat or sheep, eat some of the meat, and share the rest with the poor. Many special meat dishes are eaten so that all the family can share in the sacrifices. Sacrificing an animal as well as eating it are important, but the most vital aspect is charity. Many Kuwaitis offer a whole live animal to their servants, so they can have the prestige of offering their own sacrifice. The Bedouins bring their sheep and goats to the city to sell at this time, as they will receive the best prices. This festival was traditionally the best opportunity for the Bedouins to earn money.

Pilgrims throwing stones at three pillars in Mina, a holy place just outside Mecca. The pillars symbolize various devils. The Eid ul-Adha festival coincides with the pilgrimage to Mecca.

FOOD

MOST ENTERTAINING IN KUWAIT revolves around eating. Hospitality is a vital part of both the old Bedouin code and the life of modern Kuwaitis. Food and hospitality are inseparable for most Muslims and Arabs, and Kuwaitis are no exception to this rule. Lavish dinners and lunches at home are the most usual form of socializing for families and friends.

The traditional foods in Kuwait were those of the desert Bedouins, supplemented by a variety of fish from the Gulf. Trading, and later oil wealth, enabled Kuwaitis to develop a varied and sophisticated cuisine. Kuwaiti cuisine reflects the long history of trading contacts with other countries and consists of a mixture of Arab, Turkish, Iranian, and Indian food. There is a strong reliance on fish, rice, bread, and fruit. As there are many foreigners, most Kuwaitis are familiar with a great variety of foods. Restaurants offer a varied fare, but as all food should be *halal* ("hal-Al IL"), or food suitable for Muslims, no pork or alcohol is served.

Opposite: **Kuwaitis can choose from a wide variety of fruit, most of which are imported from around the world.**

Left: **Date palms are the most common trees in Kuwait. They provide the sweet, chewy dates that are an important part of the Gulf Arab diet. Dates can be eaten fresh or dried, softened with milk, or ground as flour.**

Fishermen with their catch for the day. Fish has always been an important part of the Kuwaiti diet because of the country's seafaring tradition.

Kuwaiti meals will usually be accompanied by bowls of tomato and garlic sauce (daqqus) and yogurt relish (rob) to cool the palate after the spicy food.

TYPICAL MEALS

Breakfast is usually eaten early, as work and school start before 8 a.m. It consists of sweet tea or coffee, bread, honey or jam, and dates. Depending on the season, lunch or dinner can be the larger meal of the day. Lunch is followed by an afternoon nap, due to the heat of the afternoon. Dinner is eaten late, when the evening cools down. Kuwaitis can sleep late and still rise early in the morning before the worst of the heat, since they take an afternoon nap.

Meals usually start with a variety of appetizers or *mezze* ("MEZ-eh"), many of which are common to the rest of the Arab world. These may include *hummous*, a smooth dip made with chickpeas and *tahini*, a paste of dried sesame seeds, garlic, salt, paprika, and lemon juice. Other popular appetizers include *falafel* (deep-fried bean croquettes), *warak al-inab* (stuffed vine leaves), and *samboosa* (pastries filled with meat, vegetables, and cheese).

FAST FOOD KUWAITI STYLE

Pizzas, hamburgers, and fried chicken are popular, especially with many young people. These food outlets are becoming places for both socializing with friends and for family outings. But fast food is unlikely to replace traditional family dining, as it has in much of America, as Kuwaitis are very attached to dining at home in large groups. Although Pizza Hut offers pepperoni pizza, there is one difference with the American version: beef pepperoni, made locally to taste just like the real thing, is used.

Kuwaitis also have their own traditional fast foods, and stalls and small shops in all areas sell kebabs, appetizers, ice cream, and juices. Sandwich bars are also popular and serve both American sandwiches and Arabic versions such as falafel.

The main course consists of chicken, lamb, rarely beef, and especially fish. Pork, of course, is never served. Fish is an important element in Kuwaiti cooking, and there are many ways of preparing it. Common fish are *hamour,* similar to sea bass, king prawns, *umm robien* (a type of lobster), and *zabedi,* a white fish unique to the Gulf. Meat, chicken, and fish are served fried, stewed, stuffed, and barbecued as kebab. Fish is often served in a curry sauce, as in India.

For very special occasions, Bedouin dishes such as whole, stuffed baby lamb cooked in milk or camel dishes are prepared. Rice is a staple of all main courses, often served decorated with almonds and raisins and flavored with meat or fish stock, saffron, and spices.

Desserts are very sweet and not usually served after a meal but as a snack at other times. Common desserts are Turkish baklava, layers of very thin pastry and nuts bathed in a sweet syrup made of sugar and rosewater. Almonds, pistachios, walnuts, raisins, cardamoms, rosewater, and saffron are common ingredients of desserts.

Fresh fruit may be served after meals, usually chilled and beautifully prepared for the guests. It would be inhospitable to have guests cut up their own fruit. Refreshing fruits such as watermelon are often served after the afternoon nap. Dates are very popular.

Coffee is an important symbol of hospitality in Arab countries. No business transaction can be concluded without tea or coffee, and coffee houses are important places for socializing.

MANNERS AND CUSTOMS

Before eating, most Kuwaitis utter the word, *bismillah*, which means "in the name of God." Afterwards they thank God for such a good meal. In modern Kuwaiti homes food is usually served at dining tables with cutlery and china. Many dining tables can seat 20 or more people. Men and women eat together in cities, unless unrelated male guests are present. For large parties, men and women often eat and entertain separately, so that the atmosphere can be more relaxed. The host always ensures that a guest has plenty to eat and his plate is never empty. It can be difficult for the guest to decline when full without offending the host who might assume that the guest is unhappy with the food.

BEDOUIN DINING

More traditional people and particularly Bedouins may eat sitting on rugs and cushions on the floor, using low tables or a tablecloth spread on the floor. They sit with one leg tucked in beneath them and the other leg with the knee raised so they can rest their arms on the knee. Men and women eat separately, with the women possibly eating after the men have finished the choicest morsels. The diners share common serving dishes, from which they eat with their fingers, having previously washed their hands. Only their right hand is used to eat, and only from that part of the dish closest to them. Pieces of large loaves of flat bread, baked on a convex tray placed over a fire, are used to pick up the food and soak up the sauces.

Bedouin food is, by necessity, very simple. Milk and milk products, such as yogurt, are a major part of the Bedouin diet, which also includes cereals such as wheat, dates, and very little meat. Animals are more useful for their milk than as meat. Foods such as soups, rice, and pulses are enriched by the addition of clarified butter. If butter is heated and then cooled, the clear liquid can be strained off and kept in a tin. Only wealthy Bedouins eat meat regularly, slaughtering a sheep or a camel to celebrate a special occasion. Fruit and vegetables, other than dates, are rare in the traditional Bedouin diet, as it is not possible to grow such things in the desert.

A man at a supermarket buying milk. Another popular beverage is a diluted yogurt drink called *laban* that is often drunk after a meal.

119

A spice market offering a wide variety of spices, which are important in Kuwaiti cooking. No two chefs can agree on the exact blend of cardamoms, cinnamon, cloves, coriander, cumin, ginger, nutmeg, pepper, and paprika found in Baharat, the most common spice mix.

FOOD PREPARATION

As many Kuwaiti dishes require lengthy preparation, most houses employ foreign servants to help with the cooking, serving, and cleaning up. Many Kuwaiti women will cook much of the food themselves, but delegate the arduous preparation to servants. The tastes and styles of the foreign servants have influenced the nature of Kuwaiti cooking greatly, making it spicier and more varied than the food of most other Arab countries.

Many Kuwaiti houses have two kitchens, one inside for preparation, snacks, tea, and coffee. The outside kitchen is ideally situated far from the living quarters, and this is where lengthy and hot baking and cooking are done. Much of Kuwaiti food has a very strong smell, and the heat generated from cooking is most unwelcome in the hot climate. Kuwaitis try to keep their houses a cool refuge from the scorching streets.

YOU BUY, WE COOK! For people who do not have an outside kitchen, most neighborhoods have small cooking shops. Manned by just one

KING PRAWN CURRY

This recipe reflects the Indian influence on Kuwaiti cooking and can be made with any shellfish or fish. The large number of spices is typical of Kuwaiti dishes. This would be served as a main course with fluffy rice and fresh bread.

12 king prawns	1 inch ($2^1/_2$ cm) fresh ginger, grated
2 tablespoons olive oil	1 level teaspoon turmeric
juice of one large lemon	1 teaspoon ground coriander
salt and black pepper	$^1/_2$ teaspoon ground cumin
3 medium onions, sliced	$^1/_2$ teaspoon chili powder
1 bay leaf	1 heaped tablespoon shredded coconut
1 stalk celery	4 medium tomatoes, skinned and chopped
2 cloves garlic, crushed	freshly chopped coriander, to garnish
$1^1/_2$ tablespoons clarified butter	

Prepare the prawns by removing the heads and shells and marinating them in olive oil and some of the lemon juice, salt, and pepper for two hours.

Put the shells in a pan with three slices of onion, the bay leaf, celery, and remaining salt and pepper, and cover with cold water. Simmer for one hour to make a rich and aromatic stock.

Sauté the garlic and remaining onion in the clarified butter until soft and transparent. Add the ginger, spices, and coconut and cook for one minute. Add chopped tomatoes and remaining lemon juice. Cook for 10 minutes.

Stir in the stock, marinade, and prawns and simmer for about 15–20 minutes, uncovered, until the prawns are tender and the sauce reduced.

Garnish with the coriander leaves.

"The unexpected guest is a gift from God."

—saying popularly believed to be Prophet Mohammed's

"The guest is King."

—popular Arab saying

These two sayings form the basic principle of Kuwaiti social life.

person and owned by immigrants, this kitchen specializes in preparing hot dishes, especially fish, according to the customer's instructions. These shops are now part of all planned housing developments. Once a fish is purchased at the market, it can be taken to this shop, where the spices to be used will be discussed. After about an hour, a phone call from the shop will let the customer know his fish dish is ready for collection.

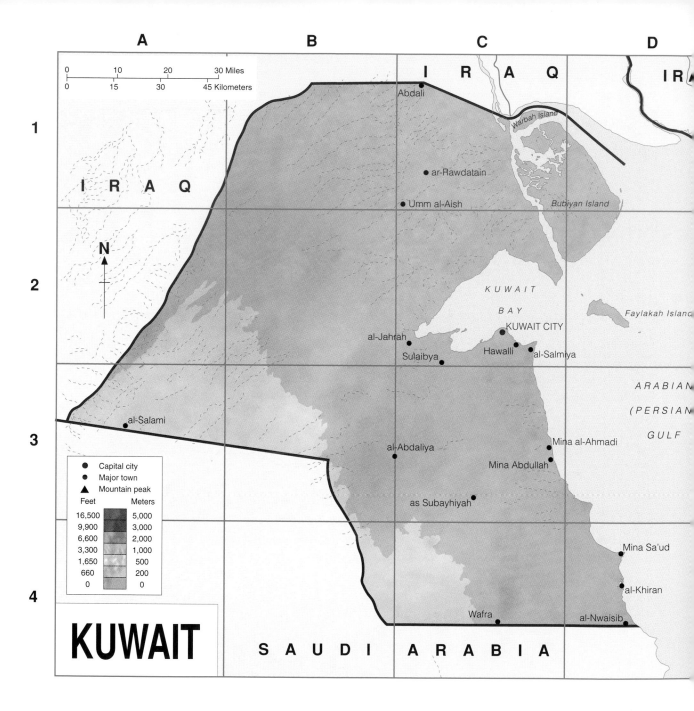

0 10 20 30 Miles
0 15 30 45 Kilometers

1

I R A Q

Abdali

Warbah Island

• ar-Rawdatain

I R A Q

• Umm al-Aish

Bubiyan Island

IR

N

2

K U W A I T

B A Y

KUWAIT CITY

Faylakah Island

al-Jahrah

Sulaibya

Hawalli ● al-Salmiya

A R A B I A N

(P E R S I A N

al-Salami

G U L F

3

al-Abdaliya

Mina al-Ahmadi

Mina Abdullah

as Subayhiyah

● Capital city
● Major town
▲ Mountain peak

Feet   Meters
16,500   5,000
9,900   3,000
6,600   2,000
3,300   1,000
1,650   500
660   200
0   0

Mina Sa'ud

al-Khiran

4

Wafra   al-Nwaisib

KUWAIT

S A U D I   A R A B I A

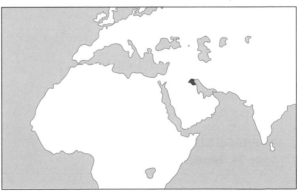

QUICK NOTES

OFFICIAL NAME
Dawlat al Kuwayt

FLAG
A rectangle, twice as long as it is wide, divided into three equal stripes—green (top), white (middle), and red (bottom). The side next to the flagpole forms the base of a black trapezoid, which protrudes into the stripes. The colors of the flag are derived from a poem by the Kuwaiti poet, Safie al-Deen al-Hili.

EMBLEM
A falcon with outspread wings embracing a dhow sailing on blue and white waves.

LAND AREA
6,880 square miles (17,819 square km)

CAPITAL CITY
Kuwait City

OTHER MAJOR CITIES
al-Jahrah, al-Salmiya

CHIEF PORT
Mina al-Ahmadi

POPULATION
1,950,047
Average annual rate of increase: 1.81%

INFANT MORTALITY RATE
11.1 per 1,000

AVERAGE LIFE EXPECTANCY
Male 74, Female 78

LITERACY RATE
79%

ETHNIC GROUPS
Kuwaiti 45%, other Arab 35%, Indian, Iranian, Pakistani

OFFICIAL LANGUAGE
Arabic

RELIGION
Islam (85%)

CURRENCY
Kuwaiti dinar, consisting of 1,000 fils
0.30 dinar = US$1

INDUSTRIES
Crude and refined oil, petrochemicals, building materials, and salt

NATURAL RESOURCES
Oil, fish, and shrimp

MAJOR EXPORTS
Crude and refined oil

MAJOR IMPORTS
Food, automobiles, building materials, machinery, and textiles

GOVERNMENT & POLITICAL LEADERS
Head of state: Emir Sheikh Jabar al-Ahmad al-Jabar al-Sabah (b. 1928), in office since 1978
Head of government: prime minister, Sheikh Saad al-Abdullah al-Salem al-Sabah (b. 1930) in office since 1978.

GLOSSARY

abbaya ("ab-BAI-yah")
A black cloak that covers the head and clothes.

agal ("ah-GAL")
Rope holding the headscarf worn by men.

Bedoon ("be-DOON")
Persons denied Kuwaiti citizenship for lack of proof that their parents or grandparents were born in Kuwait.

Bedouin ("be-DOO-een")
Desert Arab who is or was nomadic.

dhow ("dow")
Traditional Kuwaiti wooden boat.

dishdasha ("dish-DASH-ah")
Long robe worn by Kuwaiti men.

diwaniyah ("dee-WAHN-ee-yah")
Social gathering, usually for men.

Eid ul-Adha ("eed ul-ADHA")
Festival of the Sacrifice.

Eid ul-Fitr ("eed ul-FIT-reh")
Festival at the end of Ramadan.

gatra ("GAT-rah")
Scarf worn by men to cover their heads.

halal ("hal-AHL")
Food that Muslims are permitted to consume.

haram ("har-AHM")
Food forbidden to Muslims.

hejab ("he-JAHB")
Islamic covering for women.

Imam ("im-AHM")
Muslim religious leader.

Koran ("kor-AHN")
The holy book of Muslims.

masabah ("mas-AB-bah")
Worry beads.

mezze ("MEZ-eh")
Appetizers eaten before a meal.

oud ("ood")
Arab stringed instrument, like a guitar.

Ramadan ("ra-ma-DAHN")
The month of fasting and prayer.

sadu ("sa-DOO")
Traditional Bedouin weaving.

Sayyed ("say-YED")
A descendant of the Prophet Mohammed.

Sheikh ("shayk")
Honorific title for a man in Kuwait.

Sheikha ("shay-KAH")
Honorific title for a woman in Kuwait.

Shi'ite ("SHEE-ite")
Muslim minority that broke away from the main group following a leadership dispute after the death of Prophet Mohammed.

Souk ("sook")
Market.

Sunni ("SOON-ee")
The majority of Muslims belong to this sect.

BIBLIOGRAPHY

Abdul-Reda Assiri. *Kuwait's Foreign Policy: City State in World Politics*. San Francisco: Westview Press, Boulder, 1990.

Abdul-Reda Assiri. *The Government and Politics of Kuwait: Principles and Practices*. Kuwait: al-Watan Printing Press, 1996.

The Bedoons of Kuwait. Citizens without Citizenship. New York, Washington, Los Angeles: Human Rights Watch/Middle East, 1995.

Cordesman, Anthony H. *Kuwait: Recovery and Security After the Gulf War*. San Francisco: Westview Press, Boulder, 1997.

Crystal, Jill. *Kuwait: The Transformation of an Oil State*. San Francisco: Westview Press, Boulder, 1992.

Haya al-Mughani. *Women in Kuwait. The Politics of Gender*. London: Saqi Books, 1993.

Marwan Iskander. *The Cloud Over Kuwait*. New York: Vantage Press, 1991.

INDEX

INDEX

INDEX